LITERACY

Reading the Word & the World

LITERACY

Reading the Word & the World

Paulo Freire & Donaldo Macedo

ROUTLEDGE AND KEGAN PAUL
London

To Elza
whose memory
inspires hope, always

First published in 1987
This edition first published in Great Britain in 1987 by
Routledge and Kegan Paul Ltd
11 New Fetter Lane, London EC4P 4EE

Printed in Great Britain by
Biddles Ltd

ISBN 0–7102–1417–0

Contents

Foreword to this Edition
by Margaret Meek

Paulo Freire is best known for his challenging and therefore unsettling contributions to debates about theory and practice in the promotion of universal literacy. In this book he again confronts, and rejects, the assumptions of those in the dominant literate cultures who take for granted that the ability to read and write is both the cause and the effect of intellectual superiority. In so doing, he forces all teachers, whether they take responsibility for adult illiterates in the so-called Third World or teach children in primary schools anywhere, to look again at what literacy *is*. What are we helping students to learn? Why, exactly, do we think it is important that people should read and write?

These essays catch us, the favoured traditional literates, at a time of general uncertainty and paradox. In our schools we lay great emphasis on literate activities, yet we know that many of our students will make their way without too much recourse to books and papers. Nevertheless, our whole economic life is soaked in the documents of transactions, yet most of these are conducted on screens and by telephones. Freire forces us to confront uncomfortable questions; if literacy is such an obvious benefit, why are there those in literate cultures who cannot read and write? Are they not simply the dispossessed?

In all Freire's writings the core of his argument remains the same: in literacy matters, the obvious is never as obvious as it seems. Implicit in each text is the necessary, but uneasy-making interrogation: why does literacy research and practice seem to ignore the social and ideological evidence of literate behaviour which is visible in the culture itself?

When *Cultural Action for Freedom* (1970), *Pedagogy of the Oppressed* (1972) and *Education: the Practice of Freedom* (1978) were published in Britain, teachers of adult illiterates recognized in Freire someone who understood that literacy is not necessarily a universal benefit to be conferred on those who lack its advantages by those who have traditionally enjoyed them. From his point of vantage – his belonging to and identifying with the unprivileged in Latin America – Freire showed how teaching non-literate populations cannot be conceived of, nor conducted as an a-political, neutral endeavour designed by the knowledge-able rich to bring enlightenment to rural peasants or the urban poor. By mounting a critique of literacy campaigns, including those sponsored by UNESCO, Freire drew attention to the inad-equate and authoritarian nature of most attempts to provide a literacy called 'basic' or 'functional'. He showed how this thinner gruel of educational nourishment, literacy which was confining and repressive instead of enlightening and emanci-pating, had no validity for those whom he called the oppressed because it did not bring with it access to powerful means of 'speaking out' and direct access to publishing what the new literates were writing. Those who were teaching in community reading centres have recognised the situation described by Freire as that of their students, too.

When reading teachers adopt Freire's understanding that literacy must relate directly to the lives people live, and set it alongside their practical experience of teaching 'remedial' classes in school or 'special' units in community projects, they see why 'basic' education, whether in Europe or in the rapidly evolving countries, is a particular kind of insult, and that the 'back to basics' movement in education must be exposed as an unacceptable historical unreality. The notion of 'basic skills' is an educational pleonasm to divert teaching and learning from what most people experientially know about the world.

As we have learned more and more about the development of children's language and thought as interactive processes in the sharing of talk and meanings, so we have come to realize the force of Freire's primary tenets. They chime in with and complement those of Vygotsky. For both, learning involves both culturally transmitted understanding joined to the use of tools (including reading and writing) devised to enlarge one's grasp of the world for purposes which the user intends. Reading and writing are socially learned; they are sets of social practices. Freire points out the traditional societies, like ours, have educational systems which separate those who are inducted early into the acquisition of knowledge from books from those who are oriented towards a 'skills'-based approach to utilitarian texts. If we find ourselves deeply questioning this division and resisting it, there is always something of Freire's philosophy in our criticism of this state of affairs.

Here, as in the earlier books, Freire draws attention to the wider social implications of learning to read and write. When he discusses events in Nicaragua and in Guinea-Bissau he shows how literacy moves to the centre of the stage where the historical dramas of societies involved in radical evolutionary change are increasingly being played out. We can contrast this with the few occasions when, in Britain, education becomes a matter for political concern. The complaint is then made that 'standards' are 'falling': reading and writing are picked out for moral and fiscal judgment. The fact that children nowadays are writing better than at any time in the past is ignored because what they actually *say* shows independence of thought but lacks, or so it is claimed, the traditional respect for their elders embodied in the notion of 'correctness' of spelling and grammar.

What Freire has to say about the role of language in literacy is relevant beyond the sites where he encounters the problems of those peoples whose mother tongue is not the official language of the nation. If his students are to find their own voice so that they may speak or write their reading of the world, then the relation of community languages and dialects to the standard language has to be confronted. The student's own language is the means of developing a positive sense of self-worth, 'fundamental in the development of emancipatory literacy'. But Freire goes on to say, 'the goal should never be to restrict students to their own vernacular. . . . Educators should understand the value of mastering the standard dominant language of the wider society. It is through the full appropriation of the dominant standard language that students find themselves linguistically empowered to engage in dialogue with the wider sections of society.' There is nothing divisive or reductive in Freire's theory or in his practice, hence its continuing relevance to our current preoccupation with what counts as a 'model' of English that teachers are to use in their teaching of the standard forms of the language.

Freire's concern with literacy is predominantly social and political. Consequently he draws to himself the opposition of those who do not share his beliefs and those who would dismiss his idealism as romanticism. Yet, amongst teachers who have no comparable global mission in their literacy teaching, Freire is an eloquent advocate of methodologies which change the learners' view of what reading and writing are all about. When he writes as a teacher, he never loses sight of his students. In the fullest sense of education's oldest truism, he begins where they are. He foregrounds their understanding of the task they collaboratively engage in, and if he exhorts them to be critical of their reality, of the institutions and practices which shape it, it is always to enable them, as learners, to emerge from 'the culture of silence'.

No one can really judge the efficacy of Freire's admonitions who has not engaged in teaching someone to read, a child or an adult. At the beginning of this important, yet disturbing book, he gives his readers an important lesson when he writes about his own reading history. He remembers the place, the people, the texts that made up the significant events of his learning. He shows how the way he took reading and writing in hand for his own purposes and intentions before he went to school were extended and made significant when he was being taught.

> Eunice (his teacher) continued and deepened my parent' work. With her, reading the word, the phrase, the sentence, never entailed a break in reading the *world*. With her reading the word meant reading the *word-world*.

The introduction should stop here. The next move is to set Freire's ideas about literacy against our own. In my case, that of an educator of reading teachers, Freire forces me to examine the view of reading and writing which is exemplified in my practice. He supports my belief that teaching a child or an adolescent to read is not a matter of direct instruction, telling them what to do when they confront a text. In that way the words and the world remain those of the instructor. But in the dialogue of teacher and student as they read and share texts which have significance for them both, the nature of reading and writing, the importance of both for both, becomes clear. Freire makes it impossible not to ask what is literacy and why we want others to be literate. He insists that we all answer for ourselves, from our own reading of the word and the world.

MARGARET MEEK

University of London,
Institute of Education

Preface

The crisis of illiteracy has usually been relegated to Third World countries. More and more, however, illiteracy is threatening the continued development of highly industrialized nations. A much celebrated book by Jonathan Kozol, *Illiterate America* (1985), provides a succinct analysis of the illiteracy crisis in the United States, where over sixty million Americans are illiterate or functionally illiterate. The implications of a preponderantly high level of illiteracy are far-reaching and yet largely ignored. Illiteracy not only threatens the economic order of a society, it also constitutes a profound injustice. This injustice has serious consequences, such as the inability of illiterates to make decisions for themselves or to participate in the political process. Thus, illiteracy threatens the very fabric of democracy. It undermines the democratic principles of a society.

The illiteracy crisis world over, if not combatted, will further exacerbate already feeble democratic institutions and the unjust, assymetrical power relations that characterize the contradictory nature of contemporary democracies. The inherent contradiction in the actual usage of the term "democracy" is eloquently captured by Noam Chomsky, *On Power and Ideology* (1987), in his analysis of the United States society.

"Democracy," in the United States rhetoric refers to a system of governance in which elite elements based in the business community control the state by virtue of their dominance of the private society, while the population observes quietly. So understood, democracy is a system of elite decision and public ratification, as in the United States itself. Correspondingly, popular involvement in the formation of public policy is considered a serious threat. It is not a step towards democracy; rather, it constitutes a "crisis of democracy" that must be overcome.

In order to overcome, at least partly, this "crisis of democracy," a critical literacy campaign must be instituted. It must be a literacy campaign that transcends the current debate over the literacy crisis which tends to recycle old assumptions and values concerning the meaning and usefulness of literacy, that is, a notion that literacy is simply a mechanical process which overemphasizes the technical acquisition of reading and writing skills.

In *Literacy: Reading the Word, and the World,* we call for a view of literacy as a form of cultural politics. In our analysis, literacy becomes a meaningful construct to the degree that it is viewed as a set of practices that functions to either empower or disempower people. In the larger sense, literacy is analyzed according to whether it serves to reproduce existing social formation or serves as a set of cultural practices that promotes democratic and emancipatory change. In this book, we call for a concept of literacy that transcends its etymological content. That is, literacy cannot be reduced to the treatment of letters and words as purely mechanical domain. We need to go beyond this rigid comprehension of literacy and begin to view it as the relationship of learners to the world, mediated by the transforming practice of this world taking place in the very general milieu in which learners travel.

Literacy: Reading the Word, and the World is roughly divided into three parts: 1. chapters that provide a reconstructed theory of literacy as discussed in the dialogues; 2. chapters that provide concrete historical analyses of campaigns for literacy in countries such as Cape Verde, São Tome and Príncipe, and Guinea-Bissau; and 3. chapters that are informed by a language and a project of possibility that critique old views of literacy while charting new courses that point to new alternatives.

Readers are strongly urged to begin their reading of this book with Henry Giroux's introduction. Giroux situates *Literacy: Reading the Word, and the World* in a context that provides a basis for developing a critical pedagogy as related to the overall theoretical and practical implications of the book.

We would like to express our sincere thanks to Henry Giroux for his insightful comments and contributions during the preparation of the manuscript. We thank our colleagues and friends in the English Department at the University of Massachusetts at Boston for their strong support since this book was originally conceptualized, particularly Neal Bruss, Vivian Zamel, Ron Schreiber, Polly Ulichny, Eleanor Kutz, Candace Mitchell, Elsa Auerbach, and Ann Berthoff. We would also like to express appreciation to Jack Kimball and Julie Brines for their invaluable help with the copyediting of the text. We are grateful to Dale Koike for her tremendous help with the translation of parts of this book. Our thanks go the Barbara Graceffa who patiently helped with the typing and preparation of the manuscript. Finally, we thank our families for their continued strong support of our efforts to contribute to the development of a project of possibility.

PAULO FREIRE
Pontifícia Universidade Católica
São Paulo, Brazil

DONALDO MACEDO
University of Massachusetts at
Boston

Foreword
by Ann E. Berthoff

In *The Politics of Education* (1985), Paulo Freire tells us that in trying "to apprehend subjectivity and objectivity in their dialectical relationship" — of understanding, that is to say, both the promise and the limitations of what he calls "conscientization" —trying to focus his efforts, he has turned himself into "a tramp of the obvious, becoming the tramp of demystifying conscientization." He continues: "In playing the part of this vagrant I have also been learning how important the obvious becomes as the object of our critical reflection."

Paulo Freire teaches us to look — and look again — at our theory and practice and at the method we can derive from the dialectic of their relationship. Nothing in the field of literacy theory is more important than looking and looking again at the role of an awareness of awareness, of thinking about thinking, of interpreting our interpretations. Those circularities make positivists dizzy; they make those whom Freire calls "mechanicists" very impatient with the pedagogy of the oppressed. One of the things I love best about Paulo Freire is that he is restless but not impatient. That's the way it is with tramps: they love their leisure and, like Socrates, the first of that ilk, they enjoy speculative and critical dialogue in pastoral settings — but they are also constantly on the move.

Paulo Freire is once again on the move, and this activity involves, as one would expect from a master dialectician, looking again at his earlier formulations. In this book, the close successor to *The Politics of Education*, we are again offered a series of reflections and reconsiderations: three in the form of extensive dialogues with Donaldo Macedo, along with an extraordinarily interesting letter (1977) to Mario Cabral, minister of education of Guinea-Bissau, and a substantial portion of the texts of *Practice to Learn* and other workbooks prepared for the "Culture Circles" of São Tomé and Príncipe. (Some workbooks! They bespeak the principles of the pedagogy of the oppressed as brilliantly as do the lessons included in *Education for Critical Consciousness* [1973].) In commenting on the cultural context of all discourse, Freire remarks in chapter three: "I think that a pedagogy will be that much more critical and radical, the more investigative and less certain of 'certainties' it is. The more 'unquiet' a pedagogy, the more critical it will become." It's clear that he has no intention of allowing his own pedagogy to settle into "certainty." For readers who have long been familiar with Freire's theory and practice, it might appear that this sort of review would have nothing to offer, but of course that is not so. We are invited to become tramps of the obvious, and the gains are considerable.

It's instructive, then, to return to square one with Paulo Freire because his square one has always been interesting, never banal; always complex, though not complicated. The complexity is there because dialectic is there. Nothing about society or language or culture or the human soul is simple: wherever there are human beings, there is activity; and human acts are processes, and processes are dialectical. Nothing simply *unfolds*, either in nature or in history: the recalcitrance of environments and structures of all sorts is necessary to growth and development, to change and transformation. That is something obvious and it takes a good deal of tramping before we can claim an understanding.

It is fair to say that Paulo Freire's influence has been worldwide and that success in confronting the problem of illiteracy, whether in the Third World or in the inner cities of the Western world, might well depend on how those responsible for literacy programs come to understand the significance of Freire's pedagogy of the oppressed. If education is to serve other than as an instrument of oppression, it must be conceived of as a "pedagogy of knowing." Education for freedom is not simply a matter of encouraging teaching that has a political flavor; it is not a means of transmitting received ideas, no matter how "good"; it is not a matter of *extending* the teacher's knowledge to the uneducated or of informing them of the fact of their oppression. Teaching and learning are dialogic in character, and dialogic action depends on the awareness of oneself as knower, an attitude Freire calls conscientization (*conscientização*). This "critical consciousness" is informed by a philosophically sound view of language and inspirited by that unsentimental respect for human beings that only a sound philosophy of mind can assure.

In my opinion, nothing much can be made of Paulo's ideas unless two conditions are met: we study hard his philosophy of language and learning since it is fundamentally at odds with the views that have been promulgated and institutionalized (for at least forty years) by educationists, researchers, and bureaucrats alike; and we reinvent our conference and journal formats and, of course, our classrooms. I will return to this latter point, but for the time being let me sketch, particularly for the benefit of those for whom this is an introduction to Freire's work, his philosophy of language and the concept of learning it supports.

Language provides generative metaphors for Paulo Freire. His view of man as the language animal (*animal symbolicum*) is consonant with the conceptions of Whitehead, Peirce, Cassirer, Langer, and others from whom a liberation philosophy will be derived. Freire puts it this way: "The act of learning to read and write has to start from a very comprehensive understanding of the act of reading the world, something which human beings do before reading the words. Even historically, human beings first changed the world, secondly proclaimed the world and then wrote the words. These are moments of history. Human beings did not start naming A! F! N! They started by freeing the hand, grasping the world."

That was at the University of Massachusetts at Boston. In chapter three of this book, he puts it this way: "Reading the word and learning how to write the word so one can later read it are preceded by learning how to 'write' the world, that is, having the experience of changing the world and of touching the world." Freire would surely know what Emerson meant when he spoke of "the hand of the mind."

We are sometimes so used to thinking of language as a "communication medium" that it can be surprising to discover, or to be reminded, that language is the *means* of making those *meanings* that we communicate. Freire's pedagogy is founded on a philosophical understanding of this generative power of language. When we speak, the discursive power of language — its tendency towards syntax — brings thought along with it. We don't think our thoughts and then put them into words; we say and mean simultaneously. Utterance and meaning making are simultaneous and correlative. (Freire, like Vygotsky, sets aside the question of the priority of language or thought as a chicken and egg question.)

By demonstrating in the Culture Circles the role of dialogue in the making of meaning, Freire also suggests a way to set aside the fruitless debate over the "natural" character of language. The capacity for language is innate, but it can only be realized in a social setting. Peasants and teacher are engaged in dialogic action, an active exchange from which meanings emerge and *are seen to emerge*: it is central to Paulo Freire's pedagogy that learners are empowered by the knowledge that they are learners. This idea is at odds with the conventional wisdom of current educational practice which stresses that whereas *know-how* is crucially important, *knowing that* is a waste of time. The conventional model for second-language learning, as well as for the "acquisition" of "literacy skills," is motor activity. In conjunction with developmental models of cognitive growth, this view of learning legitimizes the idea of teaching as "intervention" and of theory as an authoritarian imposition.

Freire's conscientization turns these ideas on their heads. He helps us understand the full significance of the name of our species, *Homo sapiens sapiens*: man is the animal who knows that he knows. Freire argues eloquently in *Pedagogy of the Oppressed* that our species lives not only in the present moment but in history. Language gives us the power of remembering meanings and thus we can not only interpret — an animal capacity — we can also interpret our interpretations. *Knowing that* assures that there is a critical dimension of consciousness and moves us from the instinctual, unmediated, stimulus-response behavior of other animals to meaning making, to mediated activity, to making culture. Theory for Freire is the pedagogical correlative of critical consciousness; it is not inculcated but is developed and formulated as an essential activity of all learning.

Language also assures the power of envisagement: because we can name the world and thus hold it in mind, we can reflect on its meaning and imagine a changed world. Language is the means to a critical consciousness, which, in turn, is the means of conceiving of change and of making choices to bring about further transformations. Thus, naming the world transforms reality from "things" in the present moment to activities in response to situations, processes, to *becoming*. Teaching language in the context of "survival skills" is an advance over workbook drills, but it does not accomplish liberation. Liberation comes only when people reclaim their language and, with it, the power of envisagement, the imagination of a different world to be brought into being.

At the heart of Paulo Freire's pedagogy of knowing is the idea that naming the world becomes a model for changing the world. Education does not substitute for political action, but it is indispensable to it because of the role it plays in the development of critical consciousness. That, in turn, is dependent on the transforming power of language. In naming the world, the people of Freire's Culture Circles are asked to survey their farms and villages and to collect the names of tools, places, and activities that are of central importance in their lives. These "generative words" are then organized in "discovery cards," a kind of vowel grid, a do-it-yourself lexicon generator. Some words it produces are nonsense; others are recognizable. The crucial point is that sound and letter (shape) are matched with one another and with meaning or the meaning possibility. Meaning is there from the start, as it is certainly not in the case of the two competing methods of teaching reading favored by American educationists — phonics and "look-say." *Coding* and *codification* — corresponding to *what-is-said* and *what-is-meant* — are learned correlatively and simultaneously. *Decoding* — learning the relationship of letters to sounds — proceeds with *decodification* or interpretation. Meaning is thus present from the start as learners "problematize the existential." In sketches of a primitive hunter or of a squalid kitchen, or in response to a bowl of water or other codifications, they name what they see and remember, identifying and interpreting the significance of what they see.

Paulo Freire argues that for teachers simply to deride magical thinking, to try to kill off superstitious belief, is not only impossible but counterproductive. Pre-critical thought is still thought; it can and must be not simply rejected but transformed. The central task of "the adult literacy process as cultural action for freedom" is to provide the means of such transformation. The peasant — or any learner who suffers the oppression of superstition, whether of religious ideology or cold war ideology, doctrinaire liberalism or any of the multitudinous forms of totalitarian thinking — can liberate himself only by means of developing a critical consciousness.

Freire rejects the banking concept of education (the teacher makes deposits, which accumulate interest and value.) Nutrition is another metaphor: "Eat this. It's good for you!" Freire cites Sartre's sardonic salutation, "O! philosophie alimentaire!" Instead of education as extension — a reaching out to students with valuable ideas we want to share — there must be a dialogue, a dialectical exchange in which ideas take shape and change as the learners in the Culture Circle think about their thinking and interpret their interpretations. The dichotomy of "the affective" and "the cognitive," so important in American educational theory, plays no part in Freire's pedagogy. He sees thinking and feeling, along with action, as aspects of all that we do in making sense of the world.

One of the remarkable things about Paulo Freire is that he can make these ideas about the generative power of language and the role of critical consciousness accessible — and they are neither commonplace nor simple-minded. He is a master of the aphorism and of what Kenneth Burke calls the "representative anecdote," a story that points beyond itself like a metaphor. He warns against sloganeering, but mottoes and maxims are something else — and Freire is a superb phrase maker.

One should not think that reading Freire is an exercise in surveying received ideas. Even when he is setting forth conventional ideas, there are gains in significance as he develops contexts and draws implications. Paulo Freire is not only a superb theoretician; he is one of the great teachers of the century.

In this book, the principles of critical consciousness and the pedagogy of knowing again appear: they are rediscovered, reexamined, reevaluated, reinvented. *Recognition and reinvention* both centrally important in theory and practice echo throughout the pages of *Literacy: Reading the Word and the World*. Recognition entails an active critical consciousness by means of which analogies and dysanalogies are apprehended and all other acts of mind are carried out, those acts of naming and defining by means of which we make meaning. Indeed, it makes sense to say that cognition itself is contingent upon recognition, for we never simply *see*: we see *as, in terms of, with respect to, in the light of*. All such phrases signal the purposes and constraints that constitute the boundaries of "discourse" in the current use. The concept of recognition is one we must think *with* as well as *about*. One of Paulo Freire's representative anecdotes (in chapter four) illustrates how:

> . . . we visited a Culture Circle in a small fishing community called Monte Mario. They had as a generative word the term *bonito* (beautiful), the name of a fish, and as a codification they had an expressive design of the little town with its vegetation, typical houses, fishing boats in the sea, and a fisherman holding a *bonito*. The learners were looking at this codification in silence. All at once, four of them stood up as if they had agreed to do so beforehand; and they walked over to the wall where the codification was hanging. They stared at the codification closely. Then they went to the window and looked outside. They looked at each other as though they were surprised and looking again at the codification, they said: "This is Monte Mario. Monte Mario is like this and we didn't know it."

What we have here is a representation of the fundamental act of mind — *recognition*. Freire's comment on this representative anecdote is that the codification allowed the participants of the Culture Circle to "achieve some distance from their world and they began to recognize it." This interpretation of the story's meaning prepares us to recognize further that it represents the essential dialectic of all scientific investigation; it shows us how perception models concept formation; how looking and looking again is the very form and shape of creative exploration and critical thinking; how observation is the indispensable point of departure for the pedagogy of knowing. Indeed, the story is a parable of the ways of the eye of the mind, of the imagination: until the imagination is reclaimed as our human birthright, no liberation will be conceivable. The story is thus a parable of the pedagogy of knowing.

Recognition, on the part of the teacher, involves acknowledgment of what the learner knows and respect for that knowledge; it also requires evaluation. Freire realizes that to be "nonjudgmental" is a rhetorical virtue, not a logical option. We must respect the plurality of voices, the variety of discourses, and of course different languages; we must be tactful, but a neutral stance is impossible. Freire notes that all human activity is by definition purposeful and has, therefore, a direction. For a teacher not to undertake to make this direction apprehendable and to join in dialogic action to examine it is to refuse "the pedagogical, political, and epistemological task of assuming the role of a subject of that directive practice." Schoolteachers who say " 'I respect students and I am not directive and since they are individuals deserving respect, they should determine their own direction' " end up helping the power structure.

This point is very important when it comes to reinvention, which, along with recognition, is the chief theme of this book. Evaluation, direction, recognition, and articulation of purpose are not interventions, nor are they authoritarian per se. The chief reinvention that radical teachers must occasionally undertake is precisely to differentiate authority from authoritarianism and to know how to find it in all "discourses," in all meaning makers. *Respect* is the correlative of recognition, and Paulo's expression of it is always inspiriting, never question begging or sentimental. "Reinvention," he declares, in chapter seven, "requires from the reinventing subject a critical approach toward the practice and experience to be reinvented." *Criticism* for Freire always means interpreting one's interpretations, reconsidering contexts, developing multiple definitions, tolerating ambiguities so that we can learn from the attempt to resolve them. And it means the most careful attention to naming the world. Any "discourse" has embedded in it at some level the history of its purposes, but Freire continually reminds us, as well, of its heuristic (generative) character: we can ask "What if. . . ?" and "How could it be if. . . ?" By thus representing the power of envisagement, language provides the model of social transformation. When Freire writes in chapter three that "the reinvention of society . . . requires the reinvention of power," he means, I think, that reinvention is the work of the active mind; it is an act of knowing by which we reinvent our "discourse." Freire is never beguiled by utopian dreams. His dreams are formed by a critical and inventive imagination, exercised — practiced — in dialogue, in the naming and renaming of the world, which guides its remaking.

One way to remain alert to the significance of the distinctions Paulo Freire insists on is to think of them in threes. In *The Politics of Education*, he juxtaposes both the traditional church and the liberal, modernizing church "another kind of church . . . as old as Christianity itself. It is the prophetic church." That triad — *traditional/liberal-modernizing/prophetic* can serve as a paradigm of those deployed dialectically in this book; *authoritarianism/domestication/mobilization*; attitudes that are *naive/astute/critical*; and pedagogies that are *bourgeois-authoritarian-positivist/laissez faire/radically democratic*. Most provocative is one with a double middle term, the pedagogical attitudes characterized by *neutrality/manipulation or spontaneity/political praxis*. Half the controversies raging in education could be brought to an end if critical consciousness of the significance of that "or" could be developed.

Each of the chapters in this book contributes to our understanding of what is entailed in the choices we make among these triads. Those familiar with Freire's work will probably find chapter 5 of greatest interest since he discusses criticism of his work in Guinea-Bissau, especially the charge that it was "populist." "I will reflect on past reflections," Freire writes, and he proceeds with a searching analysis of what can be required of an emancipatory literacy process in a society with multiple discourses and two competing languages. The chapter all readers will find immediately enlightening, as well as entirely delightful, is the first, "The Importance of the Act of Reading." There is more wisdom in these few pages on "reading the world, reading the word" than in the so-called research cascading from psycholinguists and the agents for computer-assisted instruction, to say nothing of rhetorical theorists, who can not yet bring themselves to speak of *meaning* and *knowing* and *saying*, though they might refer gingerly to "content space" and "rhetorical space"! Positivist researchers who undertake to study literacy with "mechanicist" conceptions of language have concluded that reading the word and writing the word have no effect on cognitive capacity. My own opinion is that they are invincibly ignorant; but for those who have found such research compelling, an afternoon studying Freire's conception of *writing* as a figure for *transforming the world* would certainly be salutary and it could be prophylactic.

Three chapters are in dialogue form, and my guess is that for some readers they will be difficult to read. I think American academics — especially in the social sciences — find spoken discourse (conversation!) an alien form. Paulo and Donaldo listen to each other. They give each other feedback, saying (and really meaning) "I hear what you are saying and it seems to be this. . . ." They go on tediously, perhaps, for an impatient reader, but not for anyone who can imagine the appropriate pastoral setting or the café where these ranging, disorderly, but intensely dialogic exchanges would be listened in on. Such readers will feel that they can kibitz, can disagree or interrupt with marginal annotation. They can become virtual dialogue partners by reflecting on their own reflections.

My own experience overhearing conversations in Cambridge, Massachusetts, and on campuses across the country is that American academics keep saying "As I was saying . . ."; decoded, this means: "You interrupted me!" Such undialectical dialogues are replicated at our conferences, where we allow ourselves to be victimized by architecture, controlled by the design of meeting rooms and the schedules of maintenance staff. (Two thousand plates being stacked beyond a partition makes the encounter between two people trying to name the world a very difficult operation.) If the hotel management disallows moving the chairs around or if they want to charge thirty-five dollars apiece for extra microphones, can we not threaten to take our convention outside? Some things are more in our direct control: why is it that the favored convention genre is the lecture? Shouldn't we tramp around the obvious paradox of a *lecture* on *dialogic action*? Lectures are outmoded: why do we cling to them in our classrooms and at our conferences? The lecture is a late medieval invention instituted because books were scarce. The lecture was originally a reading (*lectito, lectere*); one man reading aloud could make a single book accessible. Why has it survived among the literate in the post-Gutenberg era? Surely, the lecture requires reinvention.

We need new models for conferences and it might well be one of Paulo Freire's gifts to us that he can help us imagine the forms our conferences might take. Here are a few procedures that could be followed without massive transformation.

1. Real panel discussions are possible if the lectern (*lectito, lectere*) can be dismantled. Three short (ten-minute) presentations followed by informal, spoken response from another three participants, who then have their turn.

2. As a variant, three participants can speak in sequence on a single topic (rehearsed spontaneity is best) with questions from the audience before they turn to the next topic.

3. Such a panel — or, indeed, a formal talk — can be followed by a scheduled ten minutes during which the audience is invited to respond *in writing*. These are gathered, a selection is made, and, with the help of information-processing equipment, made available to the participants the next day. This procedure — called "ink shedding" by its inventors, Russ Hunt and Jim Reither — moves the virtual dialogue toward actual dialogue, creating networks along the way. Technology lets us reinvent Monte Mario.

4. Scientists have developed "poster presentations" for their conventions: they are codifications of current research. A carefully formulated problem is followed by a cogent expla-

nation of an experimental procedure and a statement of the findings. Diagrams, micrographs, and other "visual aids" make the point. The scientist whose work is represented is on hand intermittently to "read" the poster and answer questions. Why haven't we done this? Why are there no poets at institutes sponsored by the National Institute of Education? Who better could develop the emblems and narratives to serve as codifications and representative anecdotes?

An unquiet pedagogy means that we must rock the boat. The simplest way to begin to do that would be to problematize the format and the function of our professional meetings. Here's an example. An admirer and close student of Paulo Freire was invited as a consultant to a meeting on literacy. He and his fellow consultant listened to the teachers (mostly black) all day as they explained in detail the standards they were ordered to uphold, the curricula they were required to plan, the tests they had to administer. When questioned, they either refused to recognize the oppressive and irrational character of these structures or they declared their powerlessness: "*They* say we have to do it." The consultant that evening consulted with his fellow consultant; they discerned a pattern: the "they" who were insisting on standards to be upheld were mostly black; "they" were insisting that (mostly) black teachers follow testing procedures with compunction, if not zeal. With a consciousness made critical by careful examination of the proceedings thus far, the consultant went to the phone and began calling superintendents: where did *this* idea about second language acquisition come from? Who is the chief source for *that* theory? Who states that *these* are the only ways? The consultant then began a second round of calls to these sources — famous linguists, famous professors (some of whom he had studied with), and famous theoreticians. They should, perhaps, have been "conference calls," but in any case that afternoon he could report verbatim from the experts: "No, that is not what I meant. No that is a misinterpretation of my research. No, that test was never intended for such a purpose. No, those are not the implications." Liberated from misinterpretation of theory, the conferees were able then to turn from problem solving (How can we raise test scores?) to problem posing (If we can define the role of writing this way, what would be the consequence for curriculum design?). The Freireista had managed to transform the conference into a Culture Circle. He had found ways of having the participants look and look again at their theory and practice until they were free to invent new pedagogies.

Paulo Freire has the audacity to believe that teachers must learn from their students in dialogue. His practice is imaginative, inventive, reinventive, and thoroughly pragmatic. Paulo Freire is one of the true heirs of William James and C. S. Peirce. He . says to us, "How your theory works and what it changes will best tell you what your theory is." He wants us to consider the worth of an idea by asking what difference it would make. He wants us to think about the dialectic of ends and means, about the mysteries of despair and hope. And he encourages us not to defer change until some propitious moment; not to waste our substance on getting people ready for change, ready to learn, ready for education, but, rather, to recognize that "the readiness is all." He reminds me of A. J. Muste, the pacifist who so annoyed Reinhold Niebuhr. Muste used to say: "There is no way to Peace; Peace is the way." I think Paulo is saying to us: "There is no way to transformation; transformation is the way." That is not mumbo-jumbo, it is not a witty paradox we should resolve: it is a dialectic we should enact.

Concord, Massachusetts

Introduction

Literacy and the Pedagogy of Political Empowerment

by Henry A. Giroux

> Each time that in one way or another, the question of language
> comes to the fore, that signifies that a series of other problems
> is about to emerge, the formation and enlarging of the ruling
> class, the necessity to establish more 'intimate' and sure relations
> between the ruling groups and the national popular masses, that
> is, the reorganisation of cultural hegemony.[1]

These remarks, made in the first half of the twentieth century
by the Italian social theorist, Antonio Gramsci, seem strangely
at odds with the language and aspirations surrounding the current conservative and liberal debate on schooling and the "problem" of literacy. In fact, Gramsci's remarks appear to both
politicize the notion of literacy and at the same time invest it
with an ideological meaning that suggests that it may have less
to do with the task of teaching people how to read and write
than with producing and legitimating oppressive and exploi-
tative social relations. A master dialectician, Gramsci viewed
literacy as both a concept and a social practice that must be
linked historically to configurations of knowledge and power,
on the one hand, and the political and cultural struggle over

language and experience on the other. For Gramsci, literacy was a double-edged sword; it could be wielded for the purpose of self and social empowerment or for the perpetuation of relations of repression and domination. As a terrain of struggle, Gramsci believed that critical literacy had to be fought for both as an ideological construct and as a social movement. As an ideology, literacy had to be viewed as a social construction that is always implicated in organizing one's view of history, the present and the future; furthermore, the notion of literacy needed to be grounded in an ethical and political project that dignified and extended the possibilities for human life and freedom. In other words, literacy as a radical construct had to be rooted in a spirit of critique and project of possibility that enabled people to participate in the understanding and transformation of their society. As both the mastery of specific skills and particular forms of knowledge, literacy had to become a precondition for social and cultural emancipation.

As a social movement, literacy was tied to the material and political conditions necessary to develop and organize teachers, community workers, and others both within and outside of schools. It was part of a larger struggle over the orders of knowledge, values, and social practices that must necessarily prevail if the fight for establishing democratic institutions and a democratic society were to succeed. For Gramsci, literacy became both a referent and mode of critique for developing forms of counterhegemonic education around the political project of creating a society of intellectuals (in the widest sense of the term) who could grasp the importance of developing democratic public spheres as part of the struggle of modern life to fight against domination as well as take an active part in the struggle for creating the conditions necessary to make people literate, to give them a voice in both shaping and governing their society.

With the exception of Paulo Freire, it is difficult in the present historical conjuncture to identify any major prominent theoretical positions or social movements that both affirm and extend the tradition of a critical literacy that has been developed in the manner of radical theorists such as Gramsci, Mikhail Bakhtin, and others.[2] In the United States, the language of literacy is almost exclusively linked to popular forms of liberal and right wing discourse that reduce it to either a functional perspective tied to narrowly conceived economic interests or to an ideology designed to initiate the poor, the underprivileged, and minorities into the logic of a unitary, dominant cultural tradition. In the first instance, the crisis in literacy is predicated on the need to train more workers for occupational jobs that demand "functional" reading and writing skills. The conservative political interests that structure this position are evident in the influence of corporate and other groups on schools to develop curricula more closely tuned to the job market, curricula that will take on a decidedly vocational orientation and in so doing reduce the need for corporations to provide on-the-job training.[3] In the second instance, literacy becomes the ideological vehicle through which to legitimate schooling as a site for character development; in this case, literacy is associated with the transmission and mastery of a unitary Western tradition based on the virtues of hard work, industry, respect for family, institutional authority, and an unquestioning respect for the nation. In short, literacy becomes a pedagogy of chauvinism dressed up in the lingo of the Great Books.

Within this dominant discourse, *illiteracy* is not merely the inability to read and write, it is also a cultural marker for naming forms of difference within the logic of cultural deprivation theory. What is important here is that the notion of cultural deprivation serves to designate in the negative sense forms of cultural currency that appear disturbingly unfamiliar and threatening when measured against the dominant culture's ideological standard regarding what is to be valorized as history, linguistic proficiency, lived experience, and standar s of community life.[4] The importance of developing a politics of difference in this view is seldom a positive virtue and attribute of public life; in fact, difference is often constituted as deficiency and is part of the same logic that defines the other within the discourse of cultural deprivation. Both ideological tendencies strip literacy from the ethical and political obligations of speculative reason and radical democracy and subjugate it to the political and pedagogical imperatives of social conformity and domination. In both cases, literacy represents a retreat from critical thought and emancipatory politics. Stanley Aronowitz has captured both the interests at work in shaping the current discourse on literacy and the problems it reproduces. He writes:

When America is in trouble it turns to its schools. . . . Employers
want an educational system closely tuned to the job market, a
system that will adjust its curriculum to their changing needs and
save them money on training. Humanists insist on the holy obligation of schools to reproduce "civilization as we know it"—
Western values, literary culture, and the skepticism of the scientific ethos. . . . At the moment, the neoconservatives have
appropriated the concept of excellence and defined it as basic
skills, technical training, and classroom discipline. Schools are
cuddling up to business and replacing any sensible notion of
literacy with something called "computer literacy." In existing
adult literacy programs, the materials and methods used reflect
an "end of ideology" approach that fails to inspire students—
and together with the stresses of everyday life—usually results
in massive dropout rates "proving" once again that most illiterates won't learn even when government money is "thrown"
at them. . . . Few are prepared to speak the traditional language
of educational humanism or fight for the idea that a general education is the basis of critical literacy. Since the collapse of the
'60s movements, progressives have me-tooed the conservatives
while radicals, with few exceptions, remain silent.[5]

If literacy has been seen as a major terrain of struggle for
conservatives and liberals, it has been only marginally embraced
by radical educational theorists.[6] When it has been incorporated
as an essential aspect of a radical pedagogy, it is gravely undertheorized, and, though displaying the best of intentions, its
pedagogical applications are often patronizing and theoretically
misleading. Literacy in this case often aims at providing working-class and minority kids with reading and writing skills that
will make them functional and critical within the school environment. In this perspective, literacy is more often than not tied
to a deficit theory of learning. The accusation is that schools
unevenly distribute particular skills and forms of knowledge so
as to benefit middle-class over working-class and minority students. At stake here is a view of literacy steeped in a notion of
equity. Literacy becomes a form of privileged cultural capital,
and subordinate groups, it is argued, deserve their distributional
share of such cultural currency. The pedagogies that often ac-
company this view of literacy stress the need for working-class
kids to learn the reading and writing skills they will need to
succeed in schools; moreover, their own cultures and experiences are often seen as strengths rather than deficits to be used

in developing a critical pedagogy of literacy. Unfortunately, the pedagogies that are developed within this assumption generally provide nothing more than a catalog-like approach of ways of using working-class culture to develop meaningful forms of instruction.

This particular approach to radical literacy is theoretically flawed for a number of reasons. First, it fails to view working-class culture as a terrain of struggle and contradiction. Secondly, it suggests that those educators working with subordinate groups need only to familiarize themselves with the histories and experiences of *their* students. There is no indication here that the culture that such students bring to the schools may be in dire need of critical interrogation and analysis. Thirdly, this approach fails to focus on the wider implications of the relationship between knowledge and power. It fails to understand that literacy is not just related to the poor or to the inability of subordinate groups to read and write adequately; it is also fundamentally related to forms of political and ideological ignorance that function as a refusal to know the limits and political consequences of one's view of the world. Viewed in this way, literacy as a process is as disempowering as it is oppressive. What is important to recognize here is the need to reconstitute a radical view of literacy that revolves around the importance of naming and transforming those ideological and social conditions that undermine the possibility for forms of community and public life organized around the imperatives of a critical democracy. This is not merely a problem associated with the poor or minority groups, it is also a problem for those members of the middle and upper classes who have withdrawn from public life into a world of sweeping privatization, pessimism, and greed. In addition, a radically reconstituted view of literacy would need to do more than illuminate the scope and nature of the meaning of illiteracy. It would also be essential to develop a programmatic discourse for literacy as part of a political project and pedagogical practice that provides a language of hope and transformation for those struggling in the present for a better future.[7]

In my view, the issue of developing an emancipatory theory of literacy along with a corresponding transformative pedagogy has taken on a new dimension and added significance in the present cold war era. Developing a cultural politics of literacy and pedagogy becomes an important starting point for enabling those who have been silenced or marginalized by the schools, mass media, cultural industry, and video culture to reclaim the authorship of their own lives. An emancipatory theory of literacy points to the need to develop an alternative discourse and critical reading of how ideology, culture, and power work within late capitalist societies to limit, disorganize, and marginalize the more critical and radical everyday experiences and common-sense perceptions of individuals. At issue here is the recognition that the political and moral gains that teachers and others have made should be held onto and fought for with a new intellectual and political rigor. For this to happen, left educators and workers at all levels of society need to assign the issue of political and cultural literacy the highest priority. Put another way, for radical literacy to come about, the pedagogical should be made more political and the political made more pedagogical. In other words, there is a dire need to develop pedagogical practices, in the first instance, that brings teachers, parents, and students together around new and more emancipatory visions of community. On the other hand, there is a need to recognize that all aspects of politics outside of the schools also represent a particular type of pedagogy, in which knowledge is always linked to power, social practices are always embodiments of concrete relations between diverse human beings and traditions, and all interaction contains implicit visions about the role of the citizen and the purpose of community. Literacy in this wider view not only empowers people through a combination of pedagogical skills and critical analysis, it also becomes a vehicle for examining how cultural definitions of gender, race, class, and subjectivity are constituted as both historical and social constructs. Moreover, literacy in this case becomes the central pedagogical and political mechanism through which to establish the ideological conditions and social practices necessary to develop social movements that recognize and fight for the imperatives of a radical democracy.

THE FREIREIAN MODEL OF EMANCIPATORY LITERACY

It is against the above considerations that Paulo Freire's previous work on literacy and pedagogy has assumed increasingly im-

portant theoretical and political significance. Historically, Paulo
Freire has provided one of the few practical and emancipatory
models upon which to develop a radical philosophy of literacy
and pedagogy. As is well known and widely documented, he
has concerned himself for the past twenty years with the issue
of literacy as an emancipatory political project, and he has developed the emancipatory content of his ideas within a concrete,
practical pedagogy. His work has exercised a significant role in
developing literacy programs not only in Brazil and Latin America, but also in Africa and in isolated programs in Europe, North
America, and Australia. Central to Freire's approach to literacy
is a dialectical relationship between human beings and the
world, on the one hand, and language and transformative
agency, on the other. Within this perspective, literacy is not
approached as merely a technical skill to be acquired, but as a
necessary foundation for cultural action for freedom, a central
aspect of what it means to be a self and socially constituted
agent. Most importantly, literacy for Freire is inherently a political project in which men and women assert their right and
responsibility not only to read, understand, and transform their
own experiences, but also to reconstitute their relationship with
the wider society. In this sense, literacy is fundamental to ag-
gressively constructing one's voice as part of a wider project of
possibility and empowerment. Moreover, the issue of literacy
and power does not begin and end with the process of learning
how to read and write critically; instead, it begins with the fact
of one's existence as part of a historically constructed practice
within specific relations of power. That is, human beings (as
both teachers *and* students) within particular social and cultural
formations are the starting point for analyzing not only how
they actively construct their own experiences within ongoing
relations of power, but also how the social construction of such
experiences provides them with the opportunity to give meaning and expression to their own needs and voices as part of a
project of self and social empowerment. Thus, literacy for Freire
is part of the process of becoming self-critical about the historically constructed nature of one's experience. To be able to name
one's experience is part of what it meant to "read" the world
and to begin to understand the political nature of the limits *and*
possibilities that make up the larger society.[8]

For Freire, language and power are inextricably intertwined and provide a fundamental dimension of human agency and social transformation. Language, as Freire defined it, plays an active role in constructing experience and in organizing and legitimating the social practices available to various groups in society. Language is the "real stuff" of culture and constitutes both a terrain of domination and field of possibility. Language, in Gramsci's terms, was both hegemonic and counterhegemonic, instrumental in both silencing the voices of the oppressed and in legitimating oppressive social relations.[9] In universalizing particular ideologies, it attempted to subordinate the world of human agency and struggle to the interests of dominant groups. But at the same time, language was also viewed as the terrain upon which radical desires, aspirations, dreams, and hopes were given meaning through a merging of the discourse of critique and possibility.

In the most immediate sense, the political nature of literacy is a fundamental theme in Freire's early writings. This is clear in his graphic portrayals of movements designed to provide Third-World people with the conditions for criticism and social action either for overthrowing fascist dictatorships or for use in postrevolutionary situations where people are engaged in the process of national reconstruction. In each case, literacy becomes a hallmark of liberation and transformation designed to throw off the colonial voice and further develop the collective voice of suffering and affirmation silenced beneath the terror and brutality of despotic regimes.

FREIRE AND MACEDO AND LITERACY AS A READING OF THE WORD AND THE WORLD

In this new book, Paulo Freire and Donaldo Macedo not only build upon the earlier work that Freire has done on literacy, they also dramatically advance and refine its implications for a broader cultural politics and extend its theoretical possibilities in further developing the basis of a critical pedagogy. The combined voices of Freire and Macedo provide a quintessential demonstration of the notion of critical literacy as an unfolding of critique and commitment through the process of dialogue.

Drawing upon their different traditions and engagements in Latin America, Africa, and the United States, Freire and Macedo situate the notions of theory and practice in a discourse that is at once historical, theoretical, and radically political. Each of these authors not only reveals his own theoretical and political voice as shaped by his respective politics and pedagogy, but each also provides a referent for the other to further interrogate and reflect upon questions that have emerged in the last decade around the meaning and significance of a radical notion of literacy based on the Freireian model. Theory and practice come together in this book in the way these two constructs are analyzed as a matter of definition and application; they are also demonstrated as a form of radical praxis in the intensely engaging dialogue carried on by Freire and Macedo. There is, for instance, an ongoing attempt to redefine the interconnections between literacy, culture, and education, to examine the issue of literacy in the United States, and to reconstruct and analyze critically the literacy program in Guinea-Bissau to which Freire provided advice and assistance. Within these dialogues, theory becomes an act of producing meaning and not merely a reiteration or recording of previously stated theoretical positions. As a result crucial new theoretical formulations and connections emerge regarding literacy, politics, and empowerment.

Freire and Macedo also analyze and demonstrate how Freire's literacy approach was given concrete political and pedagogical expression in the curriculum and literacy materials used in São Tomé and Príncipe. In this dialogue, Freire responds strongly and clearly to some of the criticisms that have been published recently regarding his work in Guinea-Bissau. This response is useful because it helps to set the historical record straight on a number of important issues and because it reveals a dialectical interaction between Freire's own normative and political principles and the formulations and strategies in which he engaged while participating in the literacy campaign in Guinea-Bissau. Freire also emerges here as a man engaged in a critical dialogue with his own ideas, his critics, and the particulars of different historical struggles. In his intelligent and sensitive efforts to engage Freire in a discussion of his work, Macedo brilliantly sets the stage for a compelling revelation of Freire the human being and Freire the revolutionary. The outcome is one that not only provides us with a broader understanding of the meaning of literacy and education as a form of cultural politics, but also demonstrates the importance of having a voice that speaks with dignity, embodies the language of critique, and engages a discourse of hope and possibility.

Rather than provide an overview in didactic fashion of the basic assumptions that inform this book, I intend to approach it in a manner consistent with its own critical and transformative spirit of viewing literacy as a effort to read the text and the world dialectically. In doing so, I want to situate Freire and Macedo's text in a theoretical framework that allows us to further understand the dialectical meaning/connection that this book has to the lived reality of teaching and pedagogy. The text in this case is represented by the critical pedagogical principles that structure the essential meaning of this book; the context is the wider world of schooling and education, including the public schools as well as those public spheres where other forms of learning and struggle exist. In what follows, I want to analyze the importance of extending literacy as both a historical and social construct for engaging the discourse of domination and for defining critical pedagogy as a form of cultural politics. I shall then suggest some of the implications Freire and Macedo's view of emancipatory literacy have for developing a radical pedagogy of voice and experience.

CRITICAL LITERACY AS A PRECONDITION FOR SELF AND SOCIAL EMPOWERMENT

In the broadest political sense, literacy is best understood as a myriad of discursive forms and cultural competencies that construct and make available the various relations and experiences that exist between learners and the world. In a more specific sense, critical literacy is both a narrative for agency as well as a referent for critique. As a narrative for agency, literacy becomes synonomous with an attempt to rescue history, experience, and vision from conventional discourse and dominant social relations. It means developing the theoretical and practical conditions through which human beings can locate themselves in their own histories and in doing so make themselves present as agents in the struggle to expand the possibilities of human life and freedom. Literacy in these terms is not the equivalent of emancipation, it is in a more limited but essential way the precondition for engaging in struggles around both relations of meaning and relations of power. To be literate is *not* to be free, it is to be present and active in the struggle for reclaiming one's voice, history, and future. Just as illiteracy does not explain the causes of massive unemployment, bureaucracy, or the growing racism in major cities in the United States, South Africa, and elsewhere, literacy neither automatically reveals nor guarantees social, political, and economic freedom.[10] As a referent for critique, literacy provides an essential precondition for organizing and understanding the socially constructed nature of subjectivity and experience and for assessing how knowledge, power, and social practice can be collectively forged in the service of making decisions instrumental to a democratic society rather than merely consenting to the wishes of the rich and the powerful.[11]

If a radical theory of literacy is to encompass human agency and critique as part of the narrative of liberation, it must reject the reductionist pedagogical practice of limiting critique to the analyses of cultural products such as texts, books, films, and other commodities.[12] Theories of literacy tied to this form of ideology critique obscure the *relational* nature of how meaning is produced, i.e., the intersection of subjectivities, objects, and social practices within specific relations of power. As such, criticism as a central dimension of this view of literacy exists at the expense of developing an adequate theory of how meaning, experience, and power are inscribed as part of a theory of human agency. Thus, central to a radical theory of literacy would be the development of a view of human agency in which the production of meaning is not limited to analyzing how ideologies are inscribed in particular texts. In this case, a radical theory of literacy needs to incorporate a notion of ideology critique that includes a view of human agency in which the production of meaning takes place in the dialogue and interaction that mutually constitute the dialectical relationship between human subjectivities and the objective world. As part of a more definitive political project, a radical theory of literacy needs to produce a view of human agency reconstructed through forms of narrative that operate as part of "a pedagogy of empowerment . . . centered within a social project aimed at the enhancement of human possibility."[13]

Central to the notion of critical literacy developed in Freire and Macedo's dialogues are a number of crucial insights regarding the politics of illiteracy. As a social construction, literacy not only names experiences considered important to a given society, it also sets off and defines through the concept of *illiterate* what can be termed the "experience of the other." The concept illiterate in this sense often provides an ideological cover for powerful groups simply to silence the poor, minority groups, women, or people of color. Consequently, naming illiteracy as part of the definition of what it means to be literate represents an ideological construction informed by particular political interests. While Freire and Macedo's interrogation of the concept illiteracy attempts to uncover these dominant ideological interests, it provides as well a theoretical basis for understanding the political nature of illiteracy as a social practice linked to both the logic of cultural hegemony and particular forms of resistance. Implicit in this analysis is the notion that illiteracy as a social problem cuts across class lines and does not limit itself to the failure of minorities to master functional competencies in reading and writing. Illiteracy signifies on one level a form of political and intellectual ignorance and on another a possible instance of class, gender, racial, or cultural resistance. As a part of the larger and more pervasive issue of cultural hegemony, illiteracy refers to the functional inability or refusal of middle- and upper-class persons to read the world and their lives in a critical and historically relational way. Stanley Aronowitz suggests a view of illiteracy as a form of cultural hegemony in his own discussion of what it should mean to be "functionally" literate.

> The real issue for the "functionally" literate is whether they can decode the messages of media culture, counter official interpretations of social, economic, and political reality; whether they feel capable of critically evaluating events, or, indeed, of intervening in them. If we understand literacy as the ability of individuals and groups to locate themselves in history, to see themselves as

social actors able to debate their collective futures, then the key obstacle to literacy is the sweeping privatization and pessimism that has come to pervade public life.[14]

Aronowitz points to the failure of most radical and critical educators to understand illiteracy as a form of cultural hegemony. Again, illiteracy as used here embodies a language and a set of social practices that underscore the need for developing a radical theory of literacy that takes seriously the task of uncovering how particular forms of social and moral regulation produce a culture of ignorance and categorical stupidity crucial to the silencing of all potentially critical voices.

It is also important to stress once again that as an act of resistance, the refusal to be literate may constitute less an act of ignorance on the part of subordinate groups than an act of resistance. That is, members of the working class and other oppressed groups may consciously or unconsciously refuse to learn the specific cultural codes and competencies authorized by the dominant culture's view of literacy. Such resistance should be seen as an opportunity to investigate the political and cultural conditions that warrant such resistance, not as unqualified acts of conscious political refusal. Simply put, the interests that inform such acts never speak for themselves, and they have to be analyzed within a more interpretative and contextual framework, one that links the wider context of schooling with the interpretation that students bring to the act of refusal. The refusal to be literate in such cases provides the pedagogical basis for engaging in a critical dialogue with those groups whose traditions and cultures are often the object of a massive assault and attempt by the dominant culture to delegitimate and disorganize the knowledge and traditions such groups use to define themselves and their view of the world.

For teachers, the central issue that needs to be investigated is the manner in which the social curriculum of schooling, as Phil Corrigan puts it, constructs social practices around the literate/illiterate differentiation so as to contribute to the

. . . regulated social construction of differential silencing and of categorized stupidity, within the vortices of sexuality, race, gender, class, language, and regionality. . . . [This] raises the centrality of the functionality of ignorance, the importance of declaring most people most of the time as unworthy, stupid, in a singular and exact guillotining and classifying word: bad. And making them "take on" this identification as if it were their only useable, exchangeable, "I.D."[15]

For Corrigan and others, the social construction of meaning within schooling is often structured through a dominating social grammar that limits the possibility for critical teaching and learning in schools. Dominant language in this case structures and regulates not only what *is* to be taught, but *how* it is to be taught and evaluated. In this analysis, ideology combines with social practice to produce a school voice—the voice of unquestioned authority—which attempts to locate and regulate the specific ways in which students learn, speak, act, and present themselves. In this sense, Corrigan is absolutely correct to argue that teaching and learning within public schooling are not merely about the reproduction of the dominant logic and ideology of capitalism. Nor are they primarily about ongoing acts of resistance waged by subordinate groups fighting for a voice and sense of dignity in the schools. Both of these social practices exist, but they are part of a much broader set of social relations in which experience and subjectivity become constructed within a variety of voices, conditions, and narratives that suggest that school represents more than compliance or rejection.

In the most general sense, schooling is about the regulation of time, space, textuality, experience, knowledge, and power amidst conflicting interests and histories that simply cannot be pinned down in simple theories of reproduction and resistance.[16] Schools must be seen in their historical and relational contexts. As institutions, they exhibit contradictory positions in the wider culture and also represent a terrain of complex struggle regarding what it means to be literate and empowered in ways that would allow teachers and students to think and act in a manner commensurate with the imperatives and reality of a radical democracy.

The task of a theory of critical literacy is to broaden our conception of how teachers actively produce, sustain, and legitimate meaning and experience in classrooms. Moreover, a theory of critical literacy necessitates a more profound understanding of how the wider conditions of the state and society produce, negotiate, transform, and bear down on the conditions of teaching so as to either enable or disable teachers from acting in a critical and transformative way. Equally important is the need to develop as a central assumption of critical literacy the recognition that knowledge is not merely produced in the heads of experts, curriculum specialists, school administrators, and teachers. The production of knowledge, as mentioned earlier, is a relational act. For teachers, this means being sensitive to the actual historical, social, and cultural conditions that contribute to the forms of knowledge and meaning that students bring to school.

If a concept of critical literacy is to be developed in conjunction with the theoretical notions of narrative and agency, then it is important that the knowledge, values, and social practices that constitute the story/narrative of schooling be understood as embodying particular interests and relations of power regarding how one should think, live, and act with regard to the past, present, and future. At its best, a theory of critical literacy needs to develop pedagogical practices in which in the battle to make sense of one's life reaffirms and furthers the need for teachers and students to recover their own voices so they can retell their own histories and in so doing "check and criticize the history [they] are told against the one [they] have lived."[17] This means more, however, than simply the retelling and comparison of stories. In order to move beyond a pedagogy of voice that suggests that all stories are innocent, it is important to examine such stories around the interest and principles that structure them and to interrogate them as part of a political project (in the widest sense) that may enable or undermine the values and practices that provide the foundation for social justice, equality, and democratic community. In its more radical sense critical literacy means making one's self present as part of a moral and political project that links the production of meaning to the possibility for human agency, democratic community, and transformative social action.[18]

LITERACY AND THE LIBERATION OF REMEMBRANCE

In their attempt to develop a model of critical literacy that embodies an ongoing dialectical relationship between a critical reading of the world and the word, Freire and Macedo establish the theoretical groundwork for a new discourse in which the notion of literacy brings with it a critical attentiveness to the web of relations in which meaning is produced both as a historical construction and as part of a wider set of pedagogical practices. Literacy in this sense means more than breaking with the predefined, or as Walter Benjamin has said, "Brushing history against the grain."[19] It also means understanding the details of everyday life and the social grammar of the concrete through the larger totalities of history and social context. As part of the discourse of narrative and agency, critical literacy suggests using history as a form of liberating memory. As used here, history means recognizing the figural traces of untapped potentialities as well as sources of suffering that constitute one's past.[20] To reconstruct history in this sense is to situate the meaning and practice of literacy in a ethical discourse that takes as its referent those instances of suffering that need to be remembered and overcome.[21]

As a liberating element of remembrance, historical inquiry becomes more than a mere preparation for the future by means of recovering a series of past events; instead, it becomes a model for constituting the radical potential of memory. It is a sober witness to the oppression and pain endured needlessly by history's victims and a text/terrain for the exercise of critical suspicion, highlighting not only the sources of suffering that need to be remembered so as not to be repeated, but also the subjective side of human struggle and hope.[22] Put another way, liberating remembrance and the forms of critical literacy it supports expresses its dialectical nature in both "its demystifying critical impulse, bearing sober witness to the sufferings of the past"[23] and in the selected and fleeting images of hope that it offers up to the present.

LITERACY AS A FORM OF CULTURAL POLITICS

Theorizing literacy as a form of cultural politics assumes that the social, cultural, political, and economic dimensions of everyday life are the primary categories for understanding contemporary schooling. Within this context, school life is not conceptualized as a unitary, monolithic, and ironclad system of rules and regulations, but as a cultural terrain characterized by the production of experiences and subjectivities amidst varying degrees of accommodation, contestation, and resistance. As a form of cultural politics, literacy both illuminates and interrogates school life as a place characterized by a plurality of conflicting languages and struggles, a site where dominant and subordinate cultures collide and where teachers, students, and school administrators often differ as to how school experiences and practices are to be defined and understood.[24] Within this type of analysis, literacy provides an important focus for understanding the political and ideological interests and principles at work in the pedagogical encounters and exchanges between the teacher, the learner, and the forms of meaning and knowledge they produce together.

At stake here is a notion of literacy that connects relations of power and knowledge not simply to *what* teachers teach but also to the productive meanings that students, in all of their cultural and social differences, bring to classrooms as part of the production of knowledge and the construction of personal and social identities. In this case, to define literacy in the Freireian sense as a critical reading of the world and the word is to lay the theoretical groundwork for more fully analyzing how knowledge is produced and subjectivities constructed within relations of interaction in which teachers and students attempt to make themselves present as active authors of their own worlds.[25]

Traditionally, radical educators have emphasized the ideological nature of knowledge (either as a form of ideology-critique or as ideologically correct content to get across to students) as the primary focus for critical educational work. Central to this perspective is a view of knowledge that suggests that it is produced in the head of the educator or teacher/theorist and not in an interactional engagement expressed through the process of writing, talking, debating, and struggling over what counts as legitimate knowledge. In short, knowledge is theoretically abstracted from its own production as part of a pedagogical encounter and is also undertheorized for the way in which it is encountered in the pedagogocial context in which it is taught to students. The notion that knowledge cannot be constructed outside of a pedagogical encounter is lost in the misconceived assumption that the truth content of knowledge is the most essential issue to be addressed in one's teaching. In this way, the relevance of the notion of pedagogy as part of a critical theory of education is either undertheorized or merely forgotten. What has often emerged from this view is a division of labor in which theorists who produce knowledge are limited to the university, those who merely reproduce it are seen as public school teachers, and those who passively receive it in bits and clumps at all levels of schooling fulfill the role of students. This refusal to develop what David Lusted has called a pedagogy of theory *and* teaching not only misrecognizes knowledge as an isolated production of meaning but also denies the knowledge and social forms out of which students give relevance to their lives and experiences. Lusted is worth repeating on this issue.

> Knowledge is not produced in the intentions of those who believe they hold it, whether in the pen or in the voice. It is produced in the process of interaction, between writer and reader at the moment of reading, and between teacher and learner at the moment of classroom engagement. Knowledge is not the matter that is offered so much as the matter that is understood. To think of fields of bodies of knowledge as if they are the property of academics and teachers is wrong. It denies an equality in the relations at moments of interaction and falsely privileges one side of the exchange, and what that side "knows," over the other. Moreover, for critical cultural producers to hold this view of knowledge carries its own pedagogy, an autocratic and elite pedagogy. It's not just that it denies the value of what learners know, which it does, but that it misrecognizes the conditions necessary for the kind of learning—critical, engaged, personal, social—called for by the knowledge itself.[26]

In the most obvious sense, this position is exemplified by teachers who define the success of their teaching exclusively through the ideological correctness of the subject matter they teach. The classic example might be the middle-class teacher who is rightly horrified at the sexism exhibited by male students in her classroom. The teacher responds by presenting students with a variety of feminist articles, films, and other curriculum materials. Rather than responding with gratitude for being po-

litically enlightened, the students respond with scorn and resistance. The teacher is baffled as the students' sexism appears
to become even further entrenched. In this encounter a number
of pedagogical and political errors emerge. First, rather than
give any attention to how the students produce meaning, the
radical teacher falsely assumes the self-evident nature of the
political and ideological correctness of her position. In doing so,
she assumes an authoritative discourse which disallows the possibility for the students to tell their own stories, to present and
then question the experiences they bring into play. Then, by
denying students the opportunity to question and investigate
the ideology of sexism as a problematic experience, the teacher
not merely undermines the voices of these students, she dis-
plays what in their eyes is just another example of institutional,
middle-class authority telling them what to think. As a result,
what appears at first to be the legitimate pedagogical intervention of a radical teacher voice ends up undermining its own
ideological convictions by ignoring the complex and fundamental relation among teaching, learning, and student culture. The
teacher's best intentions are thereby subverted by employing a
pedagogy that is part of the very dominant logic she seeks to
challenge and dismantle. What is important to recognize here
is that a radical theory of literacy needs to be constructed around
a dialectical theory of voice and empowerment. In the most
general sense this means connecting theories of teaching and
learning with wider theories of ideology and subjectivity. How
teachers and students read the world, in this case, is inextricably
linked to forms of pedagogy that can function either to silence
and marginalize students or to legitimate their voices in an effort
to empower them as critical and active citizens.[27]

Developing a radical pedagogy consistent with the view of
literacy and voice developed by Freire and Macedo also involves
rethinking the very nature of curriculum discourse. At the outset
this demands understanding curriculum as representative of a
set of underlying interests that structure how a particular story
is told through the organization of knowledge, social relations,
values, and forms of assessment. Curriculum itself represents
a narrative or voice, one that is multilayered and often contradictory but also situated within relations of power that more

often than not favor white, male, middle-class, English-speaking students. What this suggests for a theory of critical literacy and pedagogy is that curriculum in the most fundamental sense is a battleground over whose forms of knowledge, history, visions, language, culture, and authority will prevail as a legitimate object of learning and analysis.[28] Curriculum, finally, is another instance of a cultural politics whose signifying practices contain not only the logic of legitimation and domination, but also the possibility for transformative and empowering forms of pedagogy.

In addition to treating curriculum as a narrative whose interests must be uncovered and critically interrogated, radical teachers must develop pedagogical conditions in their classrooms that allow different student voices to be heard and legitimated. The type of critical pedagogy being proposed here is fundamentally concerned with student experience; it takes the problems and needs of the students themselves as its starting point. This suggests both confirming and legitimating the knowledge and experience through which students give meaning to their lives. Most obviously, this means replacing the authoritative discourse of imposition and recitation with a voice capable of speaking in one's own terms, a voice capable of listening, retelling, and challenging the very grounds of knowledge and power.[29]

It is important to stress that a critical pedagogy of literacy and voice must be attentive to the contradictory nature of student experience and voice and therefore establish the grounds whereby such experience can be interrogated and analyzed with respect to both their strengths and weaknesses. Voice in this case not only provides a theoretical framework for recognizing the cultural logic that anchors subjectivity and learning, it also provides a referent for criticising the kind of romantic celebration of student experience that characterized much of the radical pedagogy of the early 1960s. At issue here is linking the pedagogy of student voice to a project of possibility that allows students to affirm and celebrate the interplay of different voices and experience while at the same time recognizing that such voices must always be interrogated for the various ontological, epistemological, and ethical and political interests they represent. As a form of historical, textual, political, and sexual production, student voice must be rooted in a pedagogy that allows students to speak and to appreciate the nature of difference as part of both a democratic tolerance and a fundamental condition for critical dialogue and the development of forms of solidarity rooted in the principles of trust, sharing, and a commitment to improving the quality of human life. A pedagogy of critical literacy and voice needs to be developed around a politics of difference and community that is not simply grounded in a celebration of plurality. Such a pedagogy must be derived from a particular form of human community in which plurality becomes dignified through the construction of classroom social relations in which all voices in their differences become unified both in their efforts to identify and recall moments of human suffering and in their attempts to overcome the conditions that perpetuate such suffering.[30]

Secondly, a critical pedagogy must take seriously the articulation of a morality that posits a language of public life, emancipatory community, and individual and social commitment. Students need to be introduced to a language of empowerment and radical ethics that permits them to think about how community life should be constructed around a project of possibility. Roger Simon has clearly expressed this position, as follows:

> An education that empowers for possibility must raise questions of how we can work for the re-construction of social imagination in the service of human freedom. What notions of knowing and what forms of learning will support this? I think the project of possibility requires an education rooted in a view of human freedom as the understanding of necessity and the transformation of necessity. This is the pedagogy we require, one whose standards and achievement objectives are determined in relation to goals of critique and the enhancement of social imagination. Teaching and learning must be linked to the goal of educating students to take risks, to struggle with on-going relations of power, to critically appropriate forms of knowledge that exist outside of their immediate experience, and to envisage versions of a world which (in the Blochian sense) is "not-yet"—in order to be able to alter the grounds on which life is lived.[31]

Thirdly, teachers should provide students with the opportunity to interrogate different languages or ideological discourses as they are developed in an assortment of texts and curriculum materials. This is important for a number of reasons. A critical pedagogy first needs to validate and investigate the production of differential readings. In doing so, students are encouraged to engage in the theoretical and practical task of interrogating their own theoretical and political positions. Next, such a pedagogy should create the classroom conditions necessary for identifying and making problematic the contradictory and multiple ways of viewing the world that students use in constructing their view of the world. The point here is to then further develop and interrogate how students perform particular ideological operations to challenge or adopt certain positions offered in the texts and contexts available to them both in school and in the wider society. Following this, and crucial to developing a critical and dialectical understanding of voice, is the necessity for teachers to recognize that the meanings and ideologies in the text are not the only positions that can be appropriated by students.[32] Since student subjectivity and cultural identity are themselves contradictory, it is important to link how students produce meaning to the various discourses and social formations outside of schools that actively construct their contradictory experiences and subjectivities.

Fourthly, as part of the discourse of literacy and voice, critical educators need to examine the social and political interests that construct their own voices. It is especially important that teachers critically engage how such ideological interests structure their ability *both* to teach and to learn with others. A radical theory of literacy and voice must remain attentive to Freire's claim that all critical educators are also learners. This is not merely a matter of learning about what students might know; it is more importantly a matter of learning how to renew a form of self-knowledge through an understanding of the community and culture that actively constitute the lives of one's students. Dieter Misgeld puts this well:

> Social transformation includes and requires self-formation. . . . The identity of learners and teachers is just as much at issue and to be discovered through the pedagogy they cooperate in as the content of what they learn. . . . Freire's pedagogues (teacher-students or initiators of activities in culture circles) can therefore

allow themselves to learn, and they must learn from their students. The learning we speak of is not merely incidental. It is not a question of merely monitoring student performance so that a learning task can be presented with greater teaching efficiency. Rather the purpose of the educational enterprise is learned and relearned from and with the students. The students remind the teachers of the essential learning task: that learning and teaching are meant to bring about self-knowledge with knowledge of one's culture (and "the world" as Freire . . . says). One learns to understand, appreciate, and affirm membership in the culture. One is one of those for whom culture is there. One learns about oneself as a "being of decision," and "active subject of the historical process."[33]

Along with the implication that educators need to engage constantly both the word and the world is the less obvious assumption that teachers need to develop pedagogies in which teachers and students engage each other as agents of different/similar cultures. This points to how important it is for teachers to develop pedagogies that allow them to assert their own voices while still being able to encourage students to affirm, tell, and retell their personal narratives by exercising their own voices. It also suggests that the institutional and self-constituted authority that provides the basis for teacher discourse is no excuse for refusing students the opportunity to question its most basic assumptions. This is not an argument for undermining or eliminating the authority and basis for teacher voice as much as it is for providing the pedagogical basis for understanding how and why such authority is constructed and what purpose it serves. It is also important that teachers recognize how they often silence students, even when they act out of the best of intentions.[34] This suggests being critically attentive not only to the immediacy of one's voice as part of the established apparatus of power, but also to the fears, resistance, and skepticism that students from subordinate groups bring with them to the school setting.

Fifthly, the voices that structure the school environment have often been falsely theorized by left educators as part of an unbridgeable antagonism between the voice of the teacher and the school, on the one hand, and the voices of subordinate groups of students, on the other. Trapped within a polarizing logic of reproduction versus resistance, this discourse provides an inadequate understanding of how meaning is negotiated and transformed in schools; it also leaves little or no room for developing a programmatic discourse of transformation and possibility. It is to Freire and Macedo's credit that in their discussions on voice and the importance of dialogue they provide an alternative reading of what goes on in schools around the production and transformation of meaning. While the official discourse of the school and the subordinate voice of the students may be forged out of different needs, there exists a frequent interplay between the two which results in a process of mutual definition and constraint.[35] This suggests a much more subtle interaction between the dominant ideology of the schools and the ideologies of the various students who inhabit them. It should be recognized that this position advances far beyond the reproductive model of schooling developed by such different theorists as Paul Willis in England and Sam Bowles and Herb Gintis in the United States.[36] The characteristic nature of the shifting forms of accommodation, resistance, and interrogation that define the particular quality of the complex interaction between teacher and student voices cannot be overlooked, especially since it is precisely this quality that points to the importance of always analyzing dominant school culture as part of a specific historical, social, and pedagogical context. This view of voice and pedagogy also provides the basis for developing possible alliances and projects around which teachers and students can dialogue and struggle together in order to make their respective positions heard outside of their classrooms and in the larger community.

CONCLUSION

It bears repeating that the approach to literacy developed by Freire and Macedo in these pages is not simply about empowering students, it also speaks to the empowerment of teachers as part of the wider project of social and political reconstruction. Stanley Aronowitz and I have argued that critical literacy is a precondition for engaging in radical pedagogical work and social action.[37] Fundamental to this struggle is the need to redefine the nature of teachers' work and the role of teachers as transformative intellectuals. The category of intellectual is important here for analyzing both the particular ideological and material practices which structure the pedagogical relations in which teachers engage and for identifying the ideological nature of the interests which teachers produce and legitimate as part of the wider culture. The notion of intellectual provides a referent for criticizing those forms of management pedagogies, accountability schemes, and teacher-proof curricula that would define teachers merely as technicians. Moreover, it provides the theoretical and political basis for teachers to engage in a critical dialogue among themselves and others in order to fight for the conditions they need to reflect, read, share their work with others, and produce curriculum materials.

At the present time teachers in the United States are not only under attack by the new right and the federal government, they also labor under conditions overwhelmingly replete with organizational constraints and ideological conditions that leave them little room for collective work and critical pursuits. Their teaching hours are too long, they are generally isolated in cellular structures, and they have few opportunities to work collectively with their peers. Moreover, they are prevented from exercising their own knowledge with respect to the selection, organization, and distribution of teaching materials. Furthermore, teachers often operate under working conditions that are both demeaning and oppressive. This is powerfully illustrated in a recent study of Boston area elementary school teachers by Sara Freedman, Jane Jackson and Katherine Boles. They found that the rhetoric often associated with the public's view of schooling was decidedly at odds with the functions teachers were asked to perform in their jobs. For example, schools are entrusted to prepare children for adulthood, but the teachers themselves were treated as if they were incapable of making mature judgments; schools are given the responsibility to encourage a sense of autonomy and trust in students, but teachers in this study were constantly monitored within a network of administrative surveilance suggesting that they could neither be trusted nor work independently; schools are asked to create citizens capable of weighing the implications of their actions in a democratic society, yet these teachers performed within a network of work relations that was both rigidly hierarchical and sexist; even worse, they were asked to teach kids how to take risks, weigh alternatives, and exercise independent judgment while being restricted to teaching practices that emphasized the rote, mechanical, and technical aspects of learning and evaluation.[38]

It is important to emphasize strongly that teachers cannot assume the role of critical intellectuals dedicated to a pedagogy of literacy and voice unless the proper ideological and material conditions exists to support that role. Such a battle must be fought not only around the issue of *what and how* to teach, but also around the *material conditions* that enable and constrain pedagogical labor. This is both a theoretical and practical consideration that radical teachers have to address as part of a theory of critical literacy and voice. The political enormity of such a task is not meant to drive teachers to dispair as much as to suggest that by fighting for conditions that support joint teaching, collective writing and research, and democratic planning, teachers will begin to make the necessary inroads into opening new spaces for creative and reflective discourse and action. The importance of creating such a critical discourse and the conditions that support it cannot be overemphasized. For it is only within such a discourse and such practical conditions necessary to realize its interests that an emancipatory pedagogy can be developed, one that relates language and power, takes popular experiences seriously as part of the learning process, combats mystification, and helps students to reorder the raw experience of their lives through the perspectives opened up by approaches to learning based on the critical literacy model proposed by Freire and Macedo.

Of course, before schools can be constructed in ways that can empower both teachers and students, educators need to understand the present ideological and political crisis surrounding the purpose of public schooling. As part of the existing political assault on public services and social justice in general, schools are increasingly being subordinated to the imperatives of neo-conservative and right-wing interests that would make them adjuncts of the workplace or the church. In a democratic society, schools can never be reduced to company stores or training grounds for Christian fundamentalists. In this age in which democracy often seems in retreat, schools need to be recovered and fought for as democratic public spheres. More specifically, progressive educators must join with each other and with members of other social movements to fight for the importance and practice of critical literacy as part of the indispensable process of self and social formation necessary to creating forms of public life essential to the development and maintenance of a radical democracy. This suggests not only a new agenda around which to develop public school reform but also an agenda for linking divergent progressive political groups. Literacy is indispensable to all aspects of critical theory and radical praxis and should provide the basis for injecting the pedagogical back into the meaning of politics. It is to Freire and Macedo's credit that in this book they provide us with a view of literacy and voice that both demonstrate and affirm the importance of schooling as part of the struggle for expanding human possibilities within a discourse that asks new questions, reveals the importance of democratic solidarity, and advances the priority of a logic that dignifies the importance of radical democracy and social justice.

Miami University
Oxford, Ohio

The Importance of the Act of Reading[1]

In attempting to write about the importance of reading, I must say something about my preparation for being here today, something about the process of writing this book, which involved a critical understanding of the act of reading. Reading does not consist merely of decoding the written word or language; rather, it is preceded by and intertwined with knowledge of the world. Language and reality are dynamically interconnected. The understanding attained by critical reading of a text implies perceiving the relationship between text and context.

As I began writing about the importance of the act of reading, I felt myself drawn enthusiastically to rereading essential moments in my own practice of reading, the memory of which I retained from the most remote experiences of childhood, from adolescence, from young manhood, when a critical understanding of the act of reading took shape in me. In writing this book, I put objective distance between myself and the different moments at which the act of reading occurred in my experience: first, reading the world, the tiny world in which I moved; afterward, reading the word, not always the word-world in the course of my schooling.

Recapturing distant childhood as far back as I can trust my memory, trying to understand my act of *reading* the particular world in which I moved, was absolutely significant for me. Surrendering myself to this effort, I re-created and relived in the text I was writing the experiences I lived at a time when I did not yet read words.

I see myself then in the average house in Recife, Brazil, where I was born, encircled by trees. Some of the trees were like persons to me, such was the intimacy between us. In their shadow I played, and in those branches low enough for me to reach I experienced the small risks that prepared me for greater risks and adventures. The old house — its bedrooms, hall, attic, terrace (the setting for my mother's ferns), backyard — all this was my first world. In this world I crawled, gurgled, first stood up, took my first steps, said my first words. Truly, that special world presented itself to me as the arena of my perceptual activity and therefore as the world of my first reading. The *texts*, the *words*, the *letters* of that context were incarnated in a series of things, objects, and signs. In perceiving these I experienced myself, and the more I experienced myself, the more my perceptual capacity increased. I learned to understand things, objects, and signs through using them in relationship to my older brothers and sisters and my parents.

The *texts*, *words*, *letters* of that context were incarnated in the song of the birds — tanager, flycatcher, thrush — in the dance of the boughs blown by the strong winds announcing storms; in the thunder and lightening; in the rainwaters playing with geography, creating lakes, islands, rivers, streams. The *texts*, *words*, *letters* of that context were incarnated as well in the whistle of the wind, the clouds in the sky, the sky's color, its movement; in the color of foliage, the shape of leaves, the fragrance of flowers (roses, jasmine); in tree trunks; in fruit rinds (the varying color tones of the same fruit at different times — the green of a mango when the fruit is first forming, the green of a mango fully formed, the greenish-yellow of the same mango ripening, the black spots of an overripe mango — the relationship among these colors, the developing fruit, its resistance to our manipulation, and its taste). It was possibly at this time, by doing it myself and seeing others do it, that I learned the meaning of the verb *to squash.*

Animals were equally part of that context — the same way the family cats rubbed themselves against our legs, their mewing of entreaty or anger; the ill humor of Joli, my father's old black dog, when one of the cats came too near where he was eating what was his. In such instances, Joli's mood was completely different from when he rather playfully chased, caught, and killed one of the many opossums responsible for the disappearance of my grandmother's fat chickens.

Part of the context of my immediate world was also the language universe of my elders, expressing their beliefs, tastes, fears, and values which linked my world to a wider one whose existence I could not even suspect.

In the effort to recapture distant childhood, to understand my act of reading the particular world in which I moved, I re-created, relived the experiences I lived at a time when I did not yet read words. And something emerged that seems relevant to the general context of these reflections: my fear of ghosts. During my childhood, the presence of ghosts was a constant topic of grown-up conversation. Ghosts needed darkness or semidarkness in order to appear in their various forms — wailing the pain of their guilt; laughing in mockery; asking for prayers; indicating where their cask was hidden. Probably I was seven years old, the streets of the neighborhood where I was born were illuminated by gaslight. At nightfall, the elegant lamps gave themselves to the magic wand of the lamplighters. From the door of my house I used to watch the thin figure of my street's lamplighter as he went from lamp to lamp in a rhythmic gait, the lighting taper over his shoulder. It was a fragile light, more fragile even than the light we had inside the house; the shadows overwhelmed the light more than the light dispelled the shadows.

There was no better environment for ghostly pranks than this. I remember the nights in which, enveloped by my own fears, I waited for time to pass, for the night to end, for dawn's demilight to arrive, bringing with it the song of the morning birds. In morning's light my night fears sharpened my perception of numerous noises, which were lost in the brightness and bustle of daytime but mysteriously underscored in the night's deep silence. As I became familiar with my world, however, as I perceived and understood it better by *reading* it, my terrors diminished.

It is important to add that *reading* my world, always basic to me, did not make me grow up prematurely, a rationalist in boy's clothing. Exercising my boy's curiosity did not distort it, nor did understanding my world cause me to scorn the enchanting mystery of that world. In this I was aided rather than discouraged by my parents.

My parents introduced me to reading the word at a certain moment in this rich experience of understanding my immediate world. Deciphering the word flowed naturally from *reading* my particular world; it was not something superimposed on it. I learned to read and write on the ground of the backyard of my house, in the shade of the mango trees, with words from my world rather than from the wider world of my parents. The earth was my blackboard, the sticks my chalk.

When I arrived at Eunice Vascancello's private school, I was already literate. Here I would like to pay heartfelt tribute to Eunice, whose recent passing profoundly grieved me. Eunice continued and deepened my parents' work. With her, reading the word, the phrase, and the sentence never entailed a break with reading the *world*. With her, reading the word meant reading the *word-world*.

Not long ago, with deep emotion, I visited the home where I was born. I stepped on the same ground on which I first stood up, on which I first walked, began to talk, and learned to read. It was that same world that first presented itself to my understanding through my reading it. There I saw again some of the trees of my childhood. I recognized them without difficulty. I almost embraced their thick trunks — young trunks in my childhood. Then, what I like to call a gentle or well-behaved nostalgia, emanating from the earth, the trees, the house, carefully enveloped me. I left the house content, feeling the joy of someone who has reencountered loved ones.

Continuing the effort of rereading fundamental moments of my childhood experience, of adolescence and young manhood

— moments in which a critical understanding of the importance of the act of reading took shape in practice — I would like to go back to a time when I was a secondary school student. There I gained experience in the critical interpretation of texts I read in class with the Portuguese teacher's help, which I remember to this day. Those moments did not consist of mere exercises, aimed at our simply becoming aware of the existence of the page in front of us, to be scanned, mechanically and monotonously spelled out, instead of truly read. Those moments were not *reading lessons* in the traditional sense, but rather moments in which texts, including that of the young teacher Jose Pessoa, were offered to us in our restless searching.

Sometime afterward, as a Portuguese teacher in my twenties, I experienced intensely the importance of the act of reading and writing — basically inseparable — with first-year high school students. I never reduced syntactical rules to diagrams for students to swallow, even rules governing prepositions after specific verbs, agreement of gender and number, contractions. On the contrary, all this was proposed to the students' curiosity in a dynamic and living way, as objects to be discovered within the body of texts, whether the students' own or those of established writers, and not as something stagnant whose outline I described. The students did not have to memorize the description mechanically, but rather learn its underlying significance. Only by learning the significance could they know how to memorize it, to fix it. Mechanically memorizing the description of an object does not constitute knowing the object. That is why reading a text as pure description of an object (like a syntactical rule), and undertaken to memorize the description, is neither real reading nor does it result in knowledge of the object to which the text refers.

I believe much of teachers' insistence that students read innumerable books in one semester derives from a misunderstanding we sometimes have about reading. In my wanderings throughout the world there were not a few times when young students spoke to me about their struggles with extensive bibliographies, more to be *devoured* than truly read or studied, "reading lessons" in the old-fashioned sense, submitted to the students in the name of scientific training, and of which they had to give an account by means of reading summaries. In some bibliographies I even read references to specific pages in this or that chapter from such and such a book, which had to be read: "pages 15-37."

Insistence on a quantity of reading without internalization of texts proposed for understanding rather than mechanical memorization reveals a magical view of the written word, a view that must be superseded. From another angle, the same view is found in the writer who identifies the potential quality of his work, or lack of it, with the quantity of pages he has written. Yet one of the most important documents we have — Marx's "Theses on Feuerbach"— is only two and a half pages long.

To avoid misinterpretation of what I'm saying, it is important to stress that my criticism of the magical view of the word does not mean that I take an irresponsible position on the obligation we all have — teachers and students — to read the classic literature in a given field seriously in order to make the texts our own and to create the intellectual discipline without which our practice as teachers and students is not viable.

But to return to that very rich moment of my experience as a Portuguese teacher: I remember vividly the times I spent analyzing the work of Gilberto Freyre, Lins do Rego, Graciliano Ramos, Jorge Amado. I used to bring the texts from home to read with students, pointing out syntactical aspects strictly linked to the good taste of their language. To that analysis I added commentaries on the essential differences between the Portuguese of Portugal and the Portuguese of Brazil.

I always saw teaching adults to read and write as a political act, an act of knowledge, and therefore a creative act. I would find it impossible to be engaged in a work of mechanically memorizing vowel sounds, as in the exercise "ba-be-bi-bo-bu, la-le-li-lo-lu." Nor could I reduce learning to read and write merely to learning words, syllables, or letters, a process of teaching in which the teacher *fills* the supposedly *empty* heads of learners with his or her words. On the contrary, the student is the subject of the process of learning to read and write as an act of knowing and of creating. The fact that he or she needs the teacher's help, as in any pedagogical situation, does not mean that the teacher's help nullifies the student's creativity and responsibility for constructing his or her own written language and for reading this language.

When, for instance, a teacher and a learner pick up an object in their hands, as I do now, they both feel the object, perceive the felt object, and are capable of expressing verbally what the felt and perceived object is. Like me, the illiterate person can *feel* the pen, perceive the pen, and say *pen*. I can, however, not only feel the pen, perceive the pen, and say *pen*, but also write *pen* and, consequently, read *pen*. Learning to read and write means creating and assembling a written expression for what can be said orally. The teacher cannot put it together for the student; that is the student's creative task.

I need go no further into what I've developed at different times in the complex process of teaching adults to read and write. I would like to return, however, to one point referred to elsewhere in this book because of its significance for the critical understanding of the act of reading and writing, and consequently for the project I am dedicated to — teaching adults to read and write.

Reading the world always precedes reading the word, and reading the word implies continually reading the world. As I suggested earlier, this movement from the word to the world is always present; even the spoken word flows from our reading of the world. In a way, however, we can go further and say that reading the word is not preceded merely by reading the world, but by a certain form of *writing* it or *rewriting* it, that is, of transforming it by means of conscious, practical work. For me, this dynamic movement is central to the literacy process.

For this reason I have always insisted that words used in organizing a literacy program come from what I call the "word universe" of people who are learning, expressing their actual language, their anxieties, fears, demands, and dreams. Words should be laden with the meaning of the people's existential experience, and not of the teacher's experience. Surveying the word universe thus gives us the people's words, pregnant with the world, words from the people's reading of the world. We then give the words back to the people inserted in what I call "codifications," pictures representing real situations. The word *brick*, for example, might be inserted in a pictorial representation of a group of bricklayers constructing a house.

Before giving a written form to the popular word, however, we customarily challenge the learners with a group of codified situations, so they will apprehend the word rather than mechanically memorize it. Decodifying or *reading* the situations pictured leads them to a critical perception of the meaning of culture by leading them to understand how human practice or work transforms the world. Basically, the pictures of concrete situations enable the people to reflect on their former interpretation of the world before going on to read the word. This more critical reading of the prior, less critical reading of the world enables them to understand their indigence differently from the fatalistic way they sometimes view injustice.

In this way, a critical reading of reality, whether it takes place in the literacy process or not, and associated above all with the clearly political practices of mobilization and organization, constitutes an instrument of what Antonio Gramsci calls "counterhegemony."

To sum up, reading always involves critical perception, interpretation, and *rewriting* of what is read.

2

Adult Literacy and Popular Libraries

To speak of adult literacy and popular libraries is to speak of
the problems of reading and writing: not reading and writing
words in and of themselves, as if the reading and writing
of words did not imply another reading, anterior to and simultaneous with the first, the reading itself. The critical comprehension of literacy, which involves the equally critical comprehension of reading, demands the critical comprehension of reading, demands the critical comprehension of the library.
However, upon speaking of a critical vision, authenticated in a
practice of the same critical form of literacy, I not only recognize
but also emphasize the existence of a contrary practice, an understanding that, in an essay published a long time ago, I called
naive.[1]

It would be tiresome to insist on points referred to on other
occasions when I discussed the problems of literacy. Nevertheless, at the risk of repeating myself, I will try to clarify or reclarify
what I call the critical practice and understanding of literacy, as
opposed to the naive and so-called "astute" practice and un-

This chapter is adapted from a talk presented at the Eleventh Brazilian Congress
of Library Economy and Documentation, held in João Pessoa in January 1982.
It was translated by Dale A. Koike.

derstanding. The naive and astute, while identical from the objective point of view, differentiate themselves with respect to the subjectivity of their agents.

The myth of the neutrality of education — which leads to the negation of the political nature of the educational process, regarding it only as a task we do in the service of humanity in the abstract sense — is the point of departure for our understanding of the fundamental differences between a naive practice, an astute practice, and a truly critical practice.

From the critical point of view, it is as impossible to deny the political nature of the educational process as it is to deny the educational character of the political act. This does not mean, however, that the political nature of the educational process and the educational character of the political act drain the understanding of that process and this act. Just as a neutral education that claims to be at the service of humanity, of human beings in general, is impossible, so is a political practice devoid of educational meaning. But in this sense, all political parties are also always educators, and, as such, their political purpose is to win or lose souls as they denounce and issue statements. But it is in this sense, as much for the educational process as for the political act, that one of the fundamental questions arises: *in favor of whom and what* (and thus *against whom and what*) do we promote education? And *in favor of whom and what* do we develop political activity? The more we gain this clarity of understanding through practice, the more we perceive the impossibility of separating the inseparable: the education of politics. We can understand, then, that it is impossible to even think about education without considering the question of power.

It was not middle-class education that created or molded the middle class, but the middle class that, in coming to power, had the power to systematize its education. The bourgeoisie, before taking power, simply did not expect the aristocracy to give them the chance to put into practice the education they wanted. Historically, however, middle-class education began to take hold well before the middle class gained control. Its systematization and generalization were only viable once the bourgeoisie became the dominant class.

But, if from the critical point of view it is impossible to even think about education without considering the question of power, if it is impossible to understand education as an autonomous or neutral practice, this does not mean that systematic education is a pure replicator of the dominant ideology. The relations between education and subsystems and macrosystems are dynamic relations, ones that are contradictory and not mechanical. Education, it is true, reproduces the dominant ideology, but this is not the only thing it does. Even in highly modernized societies, with dominant classes that are truly competent and conscious of the role of education, education does not merely replicate dominant-class ideology. The contradictions that characterize society as it is now penetrate the intimacy of the pedgogical institutions in which systematic education is working and alter its role or its replicating work of the dominant ideology.

We perceive the impossibility of a neutral education to the extent that we understand education — on the one hand, reproducing the dominant ideology, but, on the other, independent of the intentions of one who has power, offering the negation of that ideology (or of its unveiling). Education accomplishes this through the actual, not the rhetorical, confrontation between it and reality, a reality lived by those being educated and by educators. From this moment, to speak of the impossible neutrality of education no longer frightens or intimidates us. The fact that the educator is not a neutral agent does not mean, necessarily, that he should be a manipulator. The truly liberating option is not even realized by means of a manipulative or even a spontaneous practice. Manipulation is debilitating and, likewise, irresponsible. What we as educators have to do, then, is to clarify the fact that education is political, and to be consistent with it in practice.

The question of consistency between the declared option and practice is one of the demands critical educators make on themselves. They know quite well that it is not discourse that judges practice, but practice that judges discourse. Unfortunately, many educators who proclaim a democratic option do not always have a practice consistent with such advanced discourse. Thus their discourse, inconsistent with their practice, becomes pure rhetoric. Similarly, their "inflammatory" words, contradicted by their authoritarian practice, go in one ear and out the other — the ears of Brazil's oppressed, those tired of the lack of consideration and respect that characterize their treatment by the arbitrary and arrogant people in power for the past 480 years.

Another point, characteristic of a critical view of education and literacy, is that educators have to realize that none of them is alone in the world. Each one is a being in the world, with the world and with others. To live or embody this obvious confrontation, as an educator, means to recognize in others, whether they are becoming literate or are participants in university courses, students of primary schools or members of a public assembly, the right to express their thoughts, their right to speak, which corresponds to the educator's duty to listen to them. One must listen to them attentively, with the conviction of one who completes a duty and not with the malice of one who does a favor to receive something in exchange. But since listening implies speaking, the educator has to speak to them as well. To listen to them in the sense discussed earlier is, basically, *to speak with them*, while simply speaking to them would be a way of not hearing them. A good way for educators to affirm their authoritarian elitism is to always express their thoughts to others without ever exposing and offering themselves to others, remaining arrogantly convinced that educators are here to save others. This cannot be a liberating educator's way of acting. He who scarcely speaks and never hears; he who "immobilizes" knowledge and transfers it to students, whether in primary schools or universities; he who hears only the echo of his own words, in a kind of oral narcissism; he who believes it insolent for the working class to attempt to recover its rights; he who thinks the working class is uncultured and incompetent and, thus, needs to be liberated from top to bottom — this type of educator does not really have anything to do with freedom or democracy. On the contrary, he who acts and thinks this way, consciously or unconsciously, helps to preserve the authoritarian structures.

Related to this is the need educators have to "assume" the naiveté of those becoming educated so that they will be able, with them, to overcome this naiveté. If you are walking on one side of the street, you cannot get to the other side unless you cross the street. The same thing happens with a less rigorous, less exact understanding of reality. One has to respect the levels of understanding that those becoming educated have of their own reality. To impose on them one's own understanding in the name of their liberation is to accept authoritarian solutions as ways to freedom. But to assume the naiveté of those becoming educated demands from educators a most necessary humility to assume also their ability to criticize, thus overcoming, our naiveté as well.

Only authoritarian educators deny the solidarity between the act of educating and the act of being educated by those becoming educated; only authoritarians separate the act of teaching from that of learning in such a way that he who believes himself to know actually teaches, and he who is believed to know nothing learns.

In truth, to retrieve the statement "she who knows teaches those who do not know" from its authoritarian character, it is necessary for the one who knows to understand that no one knows everything and that no one is ignorant of everything. The educator, as one who knows, first needs to recognize those being educated as the ones who are in the process of knowing more. They are the subjects of this process along with the educator and not merely accommodated patients. Second, the educator needs to recognize that knowledge is not a piece of data, something immobilized, concluded, finished, something to be transferred by one who acquired it to one who still does not possess it.

The neutrality of education, which results in being understood as a pure task, to serve in the formation of an ideal type of human being, disembodied from what is real, virtuous, and good, is one of the fundamental connotations of the naive vision of education. From the point of view of such a vision, the world is reborn in the intimacy of consciences, moved by the goodness of hearts. And since education models souls and re-creates hearts, it is the fulcrum of social change.

Before all this, however, it is necessary for education to give body and spirit to the model of the virtuous human being, leading to a beautiful and just society. Nothing can be done before an entire generation of good and just people assumes the task of creating the ideal society. But even before this generation arises, some helpful and humanitarian efforts can be realized, which can also lead to this greater project.

There are an infinite number of other characteristics of the naive vision, but space does not permit me to analyze them. I have emphasized only some of the more salient qualities so that I might focus my concerns on adult literacy. The magic character lent to the written word, seen or conceived almost like a salvationary word, is one such concern. The illiterate man, because he does not have it, is a "lost man," blind, almost outside of reality. It is necessary, then, to save him, and his salvation is in passively receiving the word as a kind of amulet — one that the "better part" of the world benevolently offers him. Thus the role of the illiterate may not be as the subject of his own illiteracy, but as the patient who submits himself passively to a process in which he cannot intervene.

From the critical and democratic point of view, as was clarified in the previous discussions, he who is becoming literate, and not the illiterate person, inserts himself into a creative process, of which he is also a subject.

From the beginning, in critical and democratic practice, the reading of the world and the word are dynamically linked. The command of reading and writing is achieved beginning with words and themes meaningful to the common experience of those becoming literate, and not with words and themes linked only to the experience of the educator. Above all, their reading of what is real cannot be the mechanically memorized repetition of our way of reading what is real. If this were so, we would fall into the same authoritarianism criticized in this book.

Earlier in this chapter I said that if, from the objective point of view, the naive identify themselves with the astute, they nevertheless distinguish themselves subjectively.[2] In truth, some of the naive objectively prevent the emancipation of the classes and oppressed social groups. Both the naive and the astute find themselves marked by the dominant, elitist ideology, but only the astute consciously assume this ideology as their own. In this sense, the latter are consciously reactionary, and thus their innocence is purely tactical. Therefore, the only difference that exists between me and an astutely naive educator with respect to the understanding of one of the central aspects of the educative process is that, while both he and I know that education is not neutral, only I affirm it.

It is important to note the difference between the nonmalicious naive person and the astute or tactical naive person. The less malicious the naiveté of a person, the more he can perceive the ineffectiveness of his actions by learning directly from his own practice. He thus renounces naiveté and, by rejecting astuteness or maliciousness, assumes a new critical posture. If before, in the stage of nontactical naiveté, the educator's attachment to the so-called poor was lyrical and idealistic, now his relationship is based on new understanding.

If social transformation was once understood in a simplistic form (that is, forming itself with a change in conscience, as if the conscience were, in fact, the transformer of what is real), now the social transformation is perceived as a historic process in which subjectivity and objectivity are united dialectically. There is no longer a way to make either objectivity or subjectivity absolute.

If adult literacy was once treated and realized in an authoritarian way, centered on the magical understanding of the word, a word bestowed by the educator on the illiterate, and if the texts generally offered students once hid much more than they revealed of reality, now literacy as an act of knowledge, as a creative act and as a political act, is an effort to read the world and the word. Now it is no longer possible to have the text without context.

On the other hand, to the very extent to which this critical educator goes about overcoming the magical and authoritarian vision of literacy, he necessarily begins to pay attention to the prevalence of oral memory. Moreover, where there is no process of infrastructural transformation under way,[3] the problem posed is not that of reading the word, but of a more rigorous reading of the world, which always precedes the reading of the word. If the masses were rarely stimulated before to write their texts, now writing is fundamental from the very beginning of literacy, so that, in the postliteracy period (when literacy has been achieved), what can come to be a small popular library can begin, with the inclusion of pages written by those who are themselves becoming educated.

It is important, upon renouncing "innocence" and rejecting

so-called astuteness or shrewdness, in the new campaign that begins with the oppressed, that all the authoritarian markings are erased. We should begin, in truth, to believe in the masses, no longer merely talking to them or about them, but listening to them, talking with them. I believe all educators, whether naive, astutely naive, or critical, learn the relevance of the popular library to the educational programs and to popular culture in general, and not only to adult literacy. Educators have a distinguished background in conceiving and putting into practice the library.

Putting aside the naive and nonastute positions, I would like to discuss the so-called astutely naive educator. From this perspective, just as the process of adult literacy is centered on bestowing, in an authoritarian manner, the dominant word and ideology upon those who are becoming literate, the popular libraries will be much more "efficient" to the degree that they help and intensify this cultural invasion. In the practice of literacy, the texts that are gradually offered during this first stage of students' growing reading capacity have little to do with the real world or the real drama of the people. Mystifying the concrete, these texts insinuate that the concrete is what is not.

From the authoritarian, elitist, reactionary point of view, the people's incompetence is almost natural. The people need to be defended because they are incapable of thinking clearly, incapable of abstracting, knowing, and creating; they are eternally "of lesser value"; and their ideas are permanently labeled exotic. Popular knowledge does not exist. The authentic manifestations of the culture of the people do not exist. The memory of their struggles needs to be forgotten, or those struggles related in a different way; the "proverbial inculture" of the people does not permit them to participate actively in the constant reinvention of their society. Those who think and act this way defend a strange democracy, a democracy that will be more "pure" and "perfect," according to them, to the degree that fewer people participate in it.

Opposed to all this is the critical-democratic position of the popular library. Reading the text in context is as important as it is in the literacy and the postliteracy efforts of adults. The popular library, as a cultural and learning center, and not just a silent depository of books, is a fundamental factor for the improvement and intensification of a correct form of reading the text in relation to the context. Reading in context implies efforts toward a correct understanding of what the written word is, the language, its relationship with the reality of one who speaks and of one who reads and writes, an understanding, then, of the relationship between reading of the world and reading of the word. Thus there is a need to have a popular library centered on this idea of reality in context, stimulating true seminars of reading, where readers seek a critical insight into the text, trying to learn its most profound meaning, proposing to the readers an aesthetic experience, involving rich resources of the popular language.

One excellent project in a rural area, developed by librarians, documentalists, educators, and historians, would be a survey of the history of the area through taped interviews, in which the older inhabitants of the area, as contemporary witnesses, would focus on the fundamental moments of their common history. Soon one would have a great quantity of stories, which would constitute a living part of the history of the area. (I found work like this being realized in Tanzania and Guinea-Bissau.) There would be narratives of famous popular figures, of the village "crazy person" (with his social importance), of the superstitions, the beliefs, the medicinal plants, of a medical doctor, of medicine men and midwives, and of poets of the people. Also there would be interviews with artists of the area: the doll makers who work with mud or wood, the sculptors, the lace makers, and the general healers who cure broken hearts or strange illnesses.

With this wealth of material, pamphlets could be published using the language — syntax, semantics, prosody — of those interviewed. These pamphlets and the recorded tapes could be used in the library itself and would be material of unquestionable value for literacy and postliteracy courses, as well other activities in the same area.

To the extent to which such research could be accomplished in different areas of the region, written and taped material could be exchanged. It is possible that in certain rural areas, to accommodate the greater level of oral communication, the popular groups might prefer to hear their friends' stories instead of reading them. There is nothing wrong with that.

One of the innumerable positive aspects of a project like this is, without a doubt, the fundamental recognition of the people's right to be the subject of research that is attempting to know them better, not the object of research that specialists do around them. In the latter case, specialists speak about them; when there are many specialists, they speak *to* the people but not *with* them. Specialists only listen as long as the people respond to the questions specialists ask.

It is clear that this kind of research demands a methodology outside the scope of this discussion, a methodology that implies recognition that the people should be the subject of the knowledge about themselves.[4]

Politics is clearly the fundamental issue in any discussion of a network of popular libraries to stimulate educational or popular culture programs (in the fields of adult literacy, health education, research, theater, technical training, and religion), programs that respond to the popular demands provoked by an effort of the popular culture.

How and what a popular library is, the composition of its stories, the activities that can be developed within its walls and then radiate outward from them — all this involves techniques, methods, processes, budgetary foresight, auxiliary personnel, and more. Yet, above all, these issues involve cultural policy. There is no neutrality, since here, too, we find degrees of the same nonastute naiveté, the same purely tactical innocence, and the same critical insights, as well as the same magical understanding of the written word, the same minimizing, reactionary elitism of the people, but also the same critical-democratic spirit that is needed in any country with a strong tradition of arbitrary resolutions.

In the chapters that follow, we will discuss in more detail these educational issues by providing a reconstructed theory of education in general, and of literacy in particular.

3

Rethinking Literacy: A Dialogue

Macedo: The notion of emancipatory literacy suggests two dimensions of literacy. On the one hand, students have to become literate about their histories, experiences, and the culture of their immediate environments. On the other hand, they must also appropriate those codes and cultures of the dominant spheres so they can transcend their own environments. There is often an enormous tension between these two dimensions of literacy. How can emancipatory literacy deal effectively with this tension so as not to suffocate either dimension?

Freire: First, I think consciousness is generated through the social practice in which we participate. But it also has an individual dimension. That is, my comprehension of the world, my dreams of the world, my judgment of the world — all of these are part of my individual practice; all speak of my presence in the world. I need all of this to begin to understand myself. But it is not sufficient to explicate my action. In the final analysis, consciousness is socially bred. In this sense, I think my subjectivity is important. But I cannot separate my subjectivity from its social objectivity.

When you ask me how to deal with the individual dimension of social consciousness, your question implies a certain relationship of tension. I believe that a critical education, an education along the lines of what Henry Giroux calls radical pedagogy, has to consider this tension and has to understand how this tension between the individual and the social practice takes place. One has to learn to deal with this relationship. In formulating a theory of education one should neither deny the social, the objective, the concrete, the material, nor emphasize only the development of the individual consciousness. In understanding the role of objectivity one must stimulate the development of the individual dimension as well.

Macedo: The fundamental question is how to deal with the individual consciousness as emphasized in an emancipatory literacy when this consciousness may be at odds with the collective social consciousness.

Freire: If you study the various ways of living and being validated in a society as complex as that of the United States, you find, for example, an undeniable taste for individualism. But the taste each person shows for individualism is that person's particular expression of a social consciousness.

Macedo: This is part of the point I wanted to address: how can one develop critical consciousness without looking at the concept of the reality of social consciousness? That is, is it possible to avoid the permanent shock that exists between individual consciousness and collective consciousness?

Freire: If we take the individualist's treatment of the social dimension, a pedagogy becomes critical when an educator like Henry Giroux or Stanley Aronowitz has a dialogue with students and methodically challenges them to discover that a critical posture necessarily implies the recognition of the relationship between objectivity and subjectivity. I would call this critical because in many cases individuals have not yet perceived themselves as conditioned; on the contrary, they passionately speak of their freedom.

When challenged by a critical educator, students begin to understand that the more profound dimension of their freedom lies exactly in the recognition of constraints that can be overcome. Then they discover for themselves in the process of becoming more and more critical that it is impossible to deny the constitutive power of their consciousness in the social practice in which they participate. On the other hand, they perceive that through their consciousness, even when they are not makers of their social reality, they transcend the constituting reality and question it. This behavioral difference leads one to become more and more critical; that is, students assume a critical posture to the extent that they comprehend how and what constitutes the consciousness of the world.

Macedo: Does the assumption of this critical posture put an end to the tension we discussed earlier?

Freire: Not at all. The tension continues. But for me, a delineated pedagogy can underscore the presence of this tension. Yet the role of critical pedagogy is not to extinguish tensions. The prime role of critical pedagogy is to lead students to recognize various tensions and enable them to deal effectively with them. Trying to deny these tensions ends up negating the very role of subjectivity. The negation of tension amounts to the illusion of overcoming these tensions when they are really just hidden.

We cannot exist outside an interplay of tensions. Even those who live passively cannot escape some measure of tensions. Frequently there is an ongoing denial of tensions, but these tensions should be understood. I believe, in fact, that one task of radical pedagogy is to clarify the nature of tensions and how best to cope with them.

Macedo: What role can a critical literacy program play in the interrelationship between productive discourse, text, and oral discourse?

Freire: It is impossible to carry out my literacy work or to understand literacy (and here I will have to repeat myself because I have no better way to answer your question) by divorcing the reading of the word from the reading of the world. Reading the word and learning how to write the word so one can later read it are preceded by learning how to write the world, that is, having the experience of changing the world and touching the world.

Macedo: How do you specifically develop the consciousness of the world in the process of literacy?

Freire: The consciousness of the world is constituted in relation to the world; it is not a part of the self. The world enables me to constitute the self in relation to "you," the world. The transformation of objective reality (what I call the "writing" of reality) represents precisely the starting point where the animal that became human began to write history. It started when these animals started to use their hands differently. As this transformation was taking place, the consciousness of the "touched" world was constituting itself. It is precisely this world consciousness, touched and transformed, that bred the consciousness of the self.

For a long time these beings, who were making themselves, wrote the world much more than they spoke the world. They directly touched and affected the world before they talked about it. Sometime later, though, these beings began to speak about the transformed world. And they began to speak about this transformation. After another long period of time, these beings began to register graphically the talk about the transformation. For this reason, I always say that before learners attempt to learn how to read and write they need to read and write the world. They need to comprehend the world that involves talk about the world.

Literacy's oral dimension is important even if it takes place in a culture like that of the United States, whose memory is preponderantly written, not oral like that of Africa, for example. Considering these different moments, which took place over millennia, and also considering the modern experience, it is not viable to separate the literacy process from general educational processes. It is not viable to separate literacy from the productive process of society. The ideal is a concomitant approach in which literacy evolves in various environments, such as the workplace. But even when literacy cannot take place in various environments, I think it is impossible to dichotomize what takes place in the economic process of the world from the process of discourse.

As to your question of whether economic discourse is an act

of production relative to acts of literacy, I would say that a critical pedagogy would have to stimulate students to reflect. Since this reflection by its very nature should be critical, learners will begin to comprehend the relationship among many different discourses. In the final analysis, these discourses are interrelated. Productive discourse and discourse about or accompanying productive discourse always intersect at some level. The problem of understanding the culture in which education takes place cannot negate the presence and influence of economic production.

Macedo: Speaking of cultural production, I would like to ask you about the relationship between education, including literacy, and culture. We have to take into account various definitions of culture, however. By "culture" I do not mean that which is representative of those dominant elements of the elite class, that is, culture with a capital C. Culture is not an autonomous system, but a system characterized by social stratification and tensions. To be precise, I have in mind Richard Johnson's definition of culture, which includes the following three main premises:

1. Cultural processes are intimately connected with social relations, especially with class relations and class formations, with sexual divisions, with the racial structuring of social relations, and with age oppressions as a form of dependency.

2. Culture involves power and helps to produce asymmetries in the abilities of individual and social groups to define and realize their needs.

3. Culture is neither autonomous nor an externally determined field, but a site of social differences and struggles.[1]

Given the range of factors that interact in cultural production and reproduction, how can an emancipatory literacy transcend social class barriers to interface with all these other factors related to culture? Can you also speak about education generally and literacy in particular as factors of culture?

Freire: Literacy and education in general are cultural expressions. You cannot conduct literacy work outside the world of culture because education in itself is a dimension of culture. Education is an act of knowledge (knowledge here is not to be restricted to a specific object only) on the part of the very subject who knows. Education has to take the culture that explains it as the object of a curious comprehension, as if one would use education to question itself. And every time that education questions itself, in response it finds itself in the larger body of culture. Evidently, the more it continues to interrogate itself about its purpose in culture and society, the more education discovers that culture is a totality cut across by social classes.

In Brazilian society, for example, one cannot deny certain behavior patterns characteristic of different social class behavior. For example, taste, which is also cultural, is heavily conditioned by social class boundaries.

Macedo: I did not intend to focus only on social classes in cultural production and reproduction. I think we need to investigate other cultural influences on education.

Freire: When a pedagogy tries to influence other factors that could not be strictly explained by a theory of class, you still have to pass through class analysis.

Given this understanding, we still must acknowledge that social classes exist and that their presence is contradictory. That is, the existence of social classes provokes a conflict of interests. It provokes and shapes cultural ways of being and, therefore, generates contradictory expressions of culture.

In general, dominant segments of any society talk about their particular interests, their tastes, their styles of living, which they regard as concrete expressions of nationality. Thus the subordinated groups, who have their own tastes and styles of living, cannot talk about their tastes and styles as national expressions. They lack the political and economic power to do so. Only those who have power can generalize and decree their group characteristics as representative of the national culture. With this decree, the dominant group necessarily depreciates all characteristics belonging to subordinated groups, characteristics that deviate from the decreed patterns.

This is especially interesting when you understand the asymmetry generated by social institutions, and how important a role critical literacy programs play in demystifying the artificial parameters imposed on people. Critical literacy has to explicate the validity of different types of music, poetry, language, and world views.

From this viewpoint the dominant class, which has the power to define, profile, and describe the world, begins to pronounce that the speech habits of the subordinate groups are a corruption, a bastardization of dominant discourse. It is in this sense that sociolinguists are making an enormous contribution to the demystification of these notions. What they show is that, scientifically, all languages are valid, systematic, rule-governed systems, and that the inferiority/superiority distinction is a social phenomenon. A language is developed to the degree that it reaches a certain stability in a particular area and to the extent that it is used in the comprehension and expression of the world by the groups that speak it.

One cannot understand and analyze a language, then, without a class analysis. Even though we may have to go beyond class boundaries to understand certain universal properties of language, we should neither reduce the investigation of language to a mechanical comprehension, nor reduce it to only social class analysis. But we have to do the latter to gain a global view of the total system under investigation.

I think all of us ultimately speak the same language (in the abstract sense) and express ourselves in different ways.

This has to do with the question you asked concerning different discourses. If you take the Brazilian case, you have the type of language spoken by the dominant class and other types spoken by workers, peasants, and similar groups. These are part of the abstract notion we call Brazilian Portuguese. This is not language as an abstraction, but language as a concrete system spoken by different groups. It is important, then, to comprehend these different varieties of language. They involve different grammars and different syntactical and semantic representations that are conditioned and explicated by people in varying positions relative to forces of production.

Language is also culture. Language is the mediating force of knowledge; but it is also knowledge itself. I believe all of this also passes through the social classes. A critical pedagogy poses this dynamic, contradictory cultural comprehension and the dynamic, contradictory nature of education as a permanent object of curiosity on the part of the learners. We find a general simplicity concerning the appreciation of these phenomena. It is as if all had been already known and decreed by the dominant groups. It is as if all that takes place at the level of culture had nothing to do with other discourses, such as the discourse of production. A pedagogy will be that much more critical and radical the more investigative and less certain of "certainties" it is. The more "unquiet" a pedagogy, the more critical it will become.

A pedagogy preoccupied with the uncertainties rooted in the issues we have discussed is, by its nature, a pedagogy that requires investigation. This pedagogy is thus much more a pedagogy of question than a pedagogy of answer.

Macedo: Let's talk about literacy as the "language of possibility," enabling learners to recognize and understand their voices within a multitude of discourses in which they must deal. How can an emancipatory literacy guarantee the legitimation of one's own discourse, which may be in a relationship of tension with other discourses? That is, if emancipatory literacy calls for the celebration of one's discourse, you will inevitably have competing discourses, all with the same goal in mind. Is it possible to have enough space within an emancipatory literacy effort to enable learners to appropriate their own discourses and simultaneously move beyond them, so as to develop competency and ease while dealing with other discourses? What roles can black American discourse, women's discourse, and the discourse of ethnic groups play in the emancipatory literacy process?

Freire: This question transcends a mechanical and strict comprehension of the reading act, that is, the act of learning the word so one can then read and write it. This question involves a dream that goes beyond the expectation of just learning to read the word. Your question implies a profound comprehension of the act of reading. To respect different discourses and to put into practice the understanding of plurality (which necessitates both criticism and creativity in the act of saying the word and in the act of reading the word) require a political and social transformation.

Your question reminds me of my dream of a different society, one in which saying the word is a fundamental right and not merely a habit, in which saying the word is the right to become a part of the decision to transform the world. To read the word that one says in this perspective presupposes the reinvention of today's society. The reinvention of society, on the other hand, requires the reinvention of power. A political perspective that only dreams of a radical change of the bourgeoisie and the seizing of power is not sufficient.

The issue is the role of subjectivity in the transformation of history. For me, historical transformation, which is part of your question, is more important than taking power. We ought not to be concerned with the mere shifting of power from one group to another. It is necessary to understand that in seizing power one must transform it. This re-creation and reinvention of power by necessity passes through the reinvention of the productive act. And the reinvention of the productive act takes place to the degree that people's discourse is legitimized in terms of people's wishes, decisions, and dreams, not merely empty words.

Discourse as a transformative act begins to assume an active and decisive participation relative to what to produce and for whom. The reinvention of power that passes through the reinvention of production cannot take place without the amplification of voices that participate in the productive act. In other words, people, not merely a minority of specialists, would have to decide on what to produce based on real necessities, not invented ones that ultimately benefit only the dominant group.

The reinvention of production, without which there would be no reinvention of power, would stimulate the reinvention of culture and the reinvention of language. Why are the majority of the people silenced today? Why should they have to muffle their own discussion? When they are called upon to read, why do they read only the dominant discourse? Literacy programs generally give people access to a predetermined and preestablished discourse while silencing their own voices, which should be amplified in the reinvention of the new society I am dreaming of. The reinvention of power that passes through the reinvention of production would entail the reinvention of culture within which environments would be created to incorporate, in a participatory way, all of those discourses that are presently suffocated by the dominant discourse.

The legitimation of these different discourses would authenticate the plurality of voices in the reconstruction of a truly democratic society. Then, in this envisioned society the comprehension of the reading act and the writing act would forcibly change. Present understanding of literacy would also have to change. By definition, there would be real respect for those learners who have not yet become familiar with saying the word to read it. This respect involves the understanding and appreciation of the many contributions nonreaders make to society in general.

You, Donaldo, told me that you are often shocked to learn that some African peoples, for example, who fought brilliantly to reappropriate their culture and throw out the colonizers, are later depreciated by the new leadership because they cannot read the word. Any people who can courageously break the chains of colonialism can also easily read the word, provided the word belongs to them. Their new leadership fails to recognize that in the struggle for liberation these people were involved in an authenic literacy process by which they learned to read their history, and that they also wrote during their struggle for liberation. This is a fundamental way to write history without writing words. It is shocking that even though they were successful in the most difficult aspect of literacy, to read and write their world, they were belittled in this much easier aspect, that which involved reading and writing the word. Your question highlights the profoundly political aspect of literacy, making me see that what you refer to as "the language of possibility" has to be based on respect for existing possibilities.

Another point that arises from your question is that of the rights of multiple voices. Taking Latin America as an example, let's think about the so-called indigenous populations. These populations were in place before the white population arrived. Thus, the white population became involved with an established civilization that also had its own voice or voices. These populations have the right to the voices that were silenced by the Hispanic-Portuguese invasion. Any literacy project for these populations necessarily would have to go through the reading of the word in their native languages. This literacy cannot require that the reading of the word be done in the colonizer's language.

If we foresee a possible revolution in these societies, we have to develop space for the literacy of possibility to take place. I remember vividly a conversation I had with Fernando Cardenal and Ernesto Cardenal in Nicaragua in which they both expressed sentiments similar to those we are now discussing. They spoke extensively about the Mosquito Indians. They both felt that in any literacy campaign, Mosquito culture had to be respected totally. Also, they felt that the Mosquitos' language would have to be a fundamental element in the literacy process. A literacy program that negates the plurality of voice and discourse is authoritarian, antidemocratic.

Macedo: Could you elaborate on the ways in which subjectivities are constituted in the schools? That is, the ways in which schools influence and shape students' ideologies, personalities, and needs.

Freire: First, I would say that schools do not really create subjectivity. Subjectivity functions within schools. Schools can and do repress the development of subjectivity, as in the case of creativity, for example. A critical pedagogy must not repress students' creativity (this is true throughout the history of education). Creativity needs to be stimulated, not only at the level of students' individuality, but also at the level of their individuality in a social context. Instead of suffocating this curious impetus, educators should stimulate risk taking, without which there is no creativity. Instead of reinforcing the purely mechanical repetitions of phrases and lists, educators should stimulate students to doubt.

Schools should never impose absolute certainties on students. They should stimulate the certainty of never being too certain, a method vital to critical pedagogy. Educators should also stimulate the possibilities of expression, the possibilities of subjectivity. They should challenge students to discourse about the world. Educators should never deny the importance of technology, but they ought not to reduce learning to a technological comprehension of the world.

We can conceive of two positions that are false here. The first would be to simplify or negate the importance of technology, to associate all technological processes with a concomitant dehumanizing process. In truth, technology represents human creativity, the expression of the necessity of risk. On the other hand, one should not fall into a denial of humanism.

The world is not made up of certainties. Even if it were, we would never know if something was really certain. The world is made of the tension between the certain and uncertain. The type of critical pedagogy I am calling for is not easy to attain in a society like that of the United States, one that has historically acquired an extraordinary advancement in technology and capital production. This extraordinary advancement has given birth to a series of myths, including the myth of technology and science. Educators should assume a scientific position that is not scientistic, a technological position that is not technologic.

Macedo: How can this critical pedagogy fundamentally stimulate the influence of subjectivity in terms of the development of students' creativity, curiosity, and needs? In societies that are technologically advanced it becomes that much more difficult to avoid falling victim to the myths to which you refer, myths that may discourage the possible role of students' subjectivities.

Freire: Yes, but at the same time these societies stimulate the role of individuality, that is, the individuality within an "individualistic" frame. The individualistic frame, in the end, also negates subjectivity. This is a curious phenomenon and we need to understand it dialectically. It could appear that a position that is profoundly individualistic would end up stimulating and respecting the role of the human agency. In truth, it denies all dimensions of human agency. Why does the individualistic position end up working against the real role of human agency? Because the only real subjectivity is that which confronts its contradictory relationship to objectivity.

And what does the individualistic position advocate? It dichotomizes the individual from the social. Generally, this cannot be accomplished, since it is not viable to do so. Nevertheless, the individualistic ideology ends up negating social interests or it subsumes social interests within individualistic interests.

The comprehension of the social is always determined by the comprehension of the individual. In this sense, the individualistic position works against the comprehension of the real role of human agency. Human agency makes sense and flourishes only when subjectivity is understood in its dialectical, contradictory, dynamic relationship with objectivity, from which it derives.

This leads to an enormous problem for critical pedagogy in technologically advanced societies. One method the critical educator can try is what you and I are doing right now, using discussion as an attempt to challenge each other so that we can understand the relationship between subjectivity and objectivity, so that we can in the final analysis understand the enormous and undeniable role of science and technology, and also so that we can understand the risk taking inherent in a humanized life. This type of discourse is one method a critical educator could use to demystify a whole network of mythology: the myth that one should not waste time, for instance. What does wasting time mean? Does one avoid wasting time only in order to make money? Or does it mean one cannot waste time making money? What is it to waste time and what is it to make time? In the end, the work of an educator in a critical and radical perspective is the work of unveiling the deep dimensions of reality that are hidden in these myths.

Macedo: You often mention the role of subject that should be assumed by students. Your preoccupation leads us to Giroux's treatment of what he calls "human agency." What do you think about the role of human agency in the dominant society regarding the complex relationship between literacy campaigns in particular and education in general?

Freire: This is one of the central themes of a radical pedagogy. It is a theme that has been accompanying the history of thought and dividing the various positions vis-à-vis the answers given. For me, this theme is another profound issue for the end of the century.

Your question brings to mind a statement by Marx. When he referred to the making of history he said that man makes history based on the concrete conditions that he finds. Evidently, it is not from the legitimate dream that a dominated class, for example, has to liberate itself. It is from concrete conditions, or more accurately, from the relationship between the concrete and the possible.

A generation inherits concrete conditions in a given society. It is from this concrete, historical situation that a generation finds it is possible to continue the continuity of history. However, the present generation has to elaborate and work on the transformation of the present concrete conditions, because without such effort it is impossible to make the future. If the present conditions are only fundamental, the present does not envelop the future within it.

For this reason the present is always a time of possibility (as Giroux has said so eloquently in his introduction to *The Politics of Education*). I think Giroux understands this perfectly when he asserts that outside the present it is impossible to make history. That is, the making of history has to take into consideration the present that came from a particular past, the base lines of this present which demarcate the making of history. When Giroux says that the present is a present possibility, not determinism, he is situating human agency in a key way, because in the relationship between the subjectivity of the present and the objectivity of the present, there is the undeniable role of subjectivity.

If subjectivity were always the result of historical transformations, objectivity would, ironically, then become the subject of the transforming subjectivity. To the extent that Giroux says that this present is a present of possibility, he is raising the issue of the role of human agency, and this is important in any critical, radical pedagogy.

Macedo: Following Giroux's discussion of public spheres' expansion of opportunities for cultivating democratic principles, to what extent do you think such areas as labor unions, the church, and social movements can be expected to play a role compatible with the goals of a critical pedagogy?

Freire: An educator who does not develop himself, who does not consider Giroux's reflections and exigencies, is out of touch with his times. In Brazil I have stressed Giroux's perspective, using a terminology that is apparently somewhat different. For example, I have insisted that a radical and critical education has to focus on what is taking place today inside various social movements and labor unions. Feminist movements, peace movements, and other such movements that express resistance generate in their practices a pedagogy of resistance. They show us that it is impossible to think of education as strictly reduced to the school environment. One cannot always deny the possibility of the schools, but we have to recognize that historically there are times when the school environment provides more or fewer opportunities.

I would say that in twenty years of military rule in Brazil there were times when there were severe repercussions if one rejected the dominant ideology. There were times when the schools were totally closed to any form of critical pedagogy. The period during the 1970s when most of the Latin American countries (for example, Uruguay, Chile, Argentina) experienced military dictatorships coincided with the emergence of Parisian theories of reproduction derived from the work of Pierre Bourdieu.[2] These theories led a number of Latin American educators to refine the possibilities of using the school environment to promote an education of resistance.

In the past four years or so, with both social and political changes in Latin America — the attempt to redemocratize Brazil, for example, or the struggle for liberation in Nicaragua — there has been a certain confidence in reestablishing the use of institutional space for experimenting with the development of a critical pedagogy.

I think, though, that even today, in an era when using the schools is possible, in order to counter the introduction of dominant ideologies, it is necessary to recognize that public environments are extremely important for pedagogical production of political and social resistance. Within this landscape of spheres of resistance, educators who seek transformation now have choices. Some may choose to work in public environments outside the schools. Others may prefer to work in their specialized fields in the schools.

I do not deny either approach. The ideal would be to establish and appreciate the relationship between these two approaches: the more traditional, structured, and systematized education that takes place in the schools versus the more dynamic, free, and contradictory (though more creative) approach within social movements. A point I developed extensively in the book I did with António Faundes[3] is that educators' comprehension of what is taking place today in these social movements and spheres of public action is most vital for critical pedagogy. Political organizations that fail to learn from the agents of these public movements will also fail to achieve historical and political resonance.

I totally agree with Giroux's view relative to the roles of public movements in the promotion of democratic principles. Giroux's critical appreciation of these movements centers on seeing them as agencies of discussion. It is within these public spheres, in fact, that antihegemonic movements have been generated. For me, the basic problem for educators and political people who dream of change lies in how to apprehend the struggle, in the sense of generating a new hegemony evolving from the manifestations and experiences within these movements.

The task of a critical educator is to approach the real world of these public spheres and social agencies, to make a contribution. An educator's major contribution would be to appreciate the theoretical elements within these movements' practices. The critical educator should make the inherent theory in these practices flourish so that people can appropriate the theories of their own practice. The role of the educator, then, is not to arrive at the level of social movements with a priori theories to explicate the practice taking place, but to discover the theoretical elements rooted in practice.

4

The People Speak Their Word: Literacy in Action[1]

I

Once again I find myself staring at a blank sheet of paper on which I am now attempting to write my thoughts about the processes of adult literacy. That I have explored this subject again and again has not in any way diminished the enthusiasm that overwhelmed me when I first began addressing it. One can never be finished with an idea as vital as adult literacy. I can think and rethink about how adults become literate and still be struck by new issues to reflect upon, even though I may not always have new things to say. I do not reflect on the purely abstract concepts of literacy, those divorced from the practice that informs them. Rather, I think about literacy in terms of the practice in which I am involved.

My thoughts in this chapter are on adult literacy in the context of the republic of São Tomé and Príncipe where, since 1976, my wife, Elza, and I have tried to contribute to adult education. But before discussing some of the central issues concerning adult literacy in Sáo Tomé and Príncipe, I would like to offer some

This chapter was translated in collaboration with Dale A. Koike.

observations on my role as a consultant to this country's government. Both Elza and I feel that a consultant is not a neutral, uncommitted person who coldly responds in a technical manner to any requests. On the contrary, we believe that a consultant's role is political and, no matter in what field, his or her practice is also political. From our point of view, it is indispensable to have an agreement between the consultant and the agency for whom he or she works.

It would be impossible for me, for example, to collaborate even minimally on a literacy campaign sponsored by a government that does not represent and act on behalf of the interests of its people. My respect for people's rights prevents me from allowing my collaboration to become a disguised "invasion" or imposition. As a prerequisite, I always make sure that the government and I share common ground. On this common ground, when identifying political options and, of course, allowing for differences of opinion, my practice renders me a colleague of the national people, never an agent who applies impossibly neutral formulae in a technical manner.

I could never be a consultant to a government that, under the guise of prioritizing learners' acquisition of reading and writing techniques, would require me (or simply suggest to me) to dichotomize reading the text from reading the context. A government for which the reading of the concrete world and the unveiling of the world are not the natural rights of the people reduces reading to a purely mechanical level.

It is precisely in this dynamic relationship between the reading of the word and the reading of reality that Elza and I found ourselves on common ground with the government of São Tomé and Príncipe. In fact, this relationship acts as a central focus of my reflections in this chapter.

All the efforts in São Tomé and Príncipe involved in the practice of adult literacy, as well as postliteracy, are oriented toward this relationship. The Popular Culture Notebooks that are being used by learners as basic texts, whether in the initial stages of literacy or in postliteracy, are not impregnated with manipulative discourses.

"Popular Culture Notebooks" is the generic name given to a series of books and primers. The first primer, for instance, is comprised of two parts. The second part is an introduction to the postliteracy phase. As a reinforcement to the first primer, there is an exercise book labeled "Practice to Learn."

The Second Popular Culture Notebook, with which one begins or learns how to begin the postliteracy phase, is written in accessible, but not simplistic, language. It treats various themes linked to the nation's present historical moment.

These texts attempt to address learners' critical curiosity and prevent readers from confronting the text in a mechanical way. (Some examples will be given in Part II of this chapter.) The language in these texts is not reduced to slogans; it is challenging. The text is designed to meet the objective of the literacy campaign, namely, for the people to participate effectively as subjects in the reconstruction of their nation.

Accordingly, these texts could not be neutral. In truth, the opposite of manipulation is learners' critical, democratic participation in the act of knowing that they are also subjects. The opposite of manipulation, in brief, is people's critical and creative participation in the process of reinventing their society, as in the case of São Tomé and Príncipe, a nation that recently freed itself from the colonial yoke to which it was subjected for centuries.

Conscious participation in the reconstruction of society takes place in most diverse sectors and at different levels of national life. It necessarily requires a critical comprehension of the nation's revolutionary transition. This critical comprehension is generated by participatory practice that actually reflects upon itself. In this sense, through generative words and themes, literacy, as well as postliteracy, cannot fail to propose to learners a critical reflection of the concrete contexts of national reality, a process that requires reflection on the present moment of reconstruction, along with challenges and difficulties to be overcome.

It is necessary, in fact, for adult literacy and postliteracy to be at the service of the nation's reconstruction and contribute to the people so that by taking more and more history into their own hands, they can shape their history. To shape history is to be present in it, not merely represented in it. Poor are those people, for example, who passively accept, without the least concern, a notice that reads: "It was decreed that on Tuesdays we begin to say good night starting at 2:00 P.M." This would be the act of a people who are represented but not present in history.

The more consciously people make their history, the more they clearly understand the difficulties in the permanent process of their liberation, difficulties that they have to confront in economic, social, and cultural domains.

To the extent that national reconstruction is the continuation of the armed struggle and past efforts to gain independence, people must assume the task of remaking their society, remaking themselves in the process. Without assuming this greater task as well as the task of remaking themselves, the people will gradually stop participating in the making of their history. This greater task thus constitutes a historical challenge of the present transitional period to the people of São Tomé and Príncipe and to the revolutionary leadership, as well. Thus, literacy and post-literacy cannot remain alien to the popular mobilization in real participatory terms. Mobilization is eminently political and pedagogical, the prime means to respond to this historical challenge. And as such, mobilization furnishes the true developmental information; it cannot be replaced by domesticating slogans focused on miniscule problems.

Adult literacy is an expression of the national reconstruction in progress. It is a political and knowing act committed in the process of learning to read and write the word and "to read" and "to write" reality. Postliteracy is an in-depth continuation of the same knowing act initiated by literacy. On the other hand, literacy and postliteracy constitute practices that stimulate reconstruction.

When an adult literacy campaign evolves around the syllabification of "ba-be-bi-bo-bu" instead of discussing the national reality with all its difficulties, and instead of raising the issue of the people's political participation in the reinvention of their society, it creates false discourses. (And this has happened in many literacy campaigns throughout the world.) It would merely represent the people of São Tomé and Príncipe in their history. On the contrary, what is taking place in São Tomé and Príncipe is the unveiling of reality. The educational approach to which the government has committed itself unmasks the truth; it does not hide the truth to benefit the ruling class.

The basic themes of this literacy campaign are:

- comprehension of the work process and the productive act in its complexity;
- ways to organize and to develop production;
- the need for technical training (which is not reduced to a narrow, alienating specialization);
- comprehension of culture and its role, not only in the process of liberation, but also in national reconstruction;
- problems of cultural identity, whose defense should not mean the ingenuous rejection of other cultures' contributions.

All of these are fundamental themes to which the majority of words in literacy training refer.

These themes are to be debated, whenever possible, as the introduction of an initial literacy phase; and they are to be introduced more problematically in the texts of the Popular Culture Notebooks of postliteracy.

As I gradually fill the empty pages of this chapter, I think back to São Tomé and picture myself visiting the Cultural Circles in rural and urban areas, always accompanied by my friends, the coordinators of the adult literacy campaign. During these visits, along with some failures, we discovered the most positive aspects of participants' political and pedagogical practices, that is the groups' intellectual development, their capacity to read texts and to comprehend reality. One time we visited a Cultural Circle in a small fishing community called Monte Mario. They had as a generative word the term *bonito* (beautiful), the name of a fish, and as a codification they had an expressive design of the little town with its vegetation, typical houses, fishing boats in the sea, and a fisherman holding a *bonito*. The learners were looking at this codification in silence. All at once, four of them stood up, as if they had agreed to do so beforehand, and walked over to the wall where the codification was hanging. They stared at the codification closely. Then they went to the window and looked outside. They looked at each other as though they were surprised, and looking again at the codification, they said: "This is Monte Mario. Monte Mario is like this and we didn't know it." Through the codification these participants could achieve some distance from their world and they began to recognize it. It was as if they were emerging from their world to know it better. In the Cultural Circle later that afternoon they had a different experience. They broke through their strict intimacy with Monte Mario and, as observing subjects, put themselves face to face with the small world of their existence.

In these Cultural Circles (the context that I sometimes refer to as theoretical), the attitude of a curious and critical subject is a fundamental point of departure for the literacy process. Reality in the process of transformation and the exercise of this critical activity in the analysis of social practice make it possible for learners to penetrate more deeply into the act of knowing in the postliteracy phase and to assume a more curious attitude toward their own way of life. This critical attitude is characterized by one who is always questioning one's own experience, as well as the reasoning behind this experience.

In the literacy phase, what is attempted is not a profound comprehension of reality under analysis, but the development of a curious attitude to stimulate learners' critical capacity as subjects of knowledge who are challenged by the object to be known. What is important is the systematic experience of this relationship between the subject who searches and the object to be known. This relationship does not exist when learners are regarded as patients of the practice, mere recipients of educators' words. In this case, learners do not say their own words.

Obviously not everything is rosy in the development of a project such as this. This is especially so in a small country that has only recently gained its independence. Its people and leadership have had to confront enormous difficulties, for instance, price fluctuations on the international market for cocoa, its principal commodity. Nor is it easy to overcome the negative legacy of centuries of colonialism, characterized by the lack of trained personnel to carry out the tasks required in national reconstruction.

The lack of trained personnel and material resources, naturally enough reflected in adult literacy, were obstacles not only in planning but also in the implementation of the literacy program. It was for this reason, then, that the former minister of education, Maria Amorim, opted for a modest yet realistic program, a program to be implemented over four years, with the hope of eradicating illiteracy in São Tomé and Príncipe while the people learned to say their word.

II

Several times in Part I of this chapter I said that the materials developed for both the literacy and postliteracy phases should be challenging and not patronizing. To show how this was done in São Tomé and in Príncipe, parts of the Exercise Workbook "Practice to Learn," of the literacy phase, and some texts of the Second Popular Culture Notebook, of the postliteracy stage, will be excerpted here.[2]

The first stage of "Practice to Learn" is comprised of two codifications (photographs): the first, a photo of one of the beautiful coves of São Tomé, with a group of young people swimming; the second, a photo of a rural area, with a group of youths working. Next to the picture of the youths swimming is written: "It is by swimming that one learns to swim." Next to the picture of the youths working is written: "It is by working that one learns to work." And at the bottom of the page: "By practicing, we learn to practice better."

The first page of the Exercise Workbook (which is used when those becoming literate are already capable of reading short sentences) offers the educator and those being educated a reflection on the importance of practice in gaining knowledge. Reinforced here is the fundamental idea that one has knowledge to the extent that one reacts by participating in a practice that is social.

The second page of the Workbook reinforces the importance of practice. It reads:

If it is by practicing that one learns to swim,
If it is by practicing that one learns to work,
And also if it is by practicing that one learns to read and write,
Let's practice to learn
and learn in order to practice better.

Let's read:
    People
    Health
    *Matabala**
    Radio
    Let's write:

The blank space that follows this passage is for the use of those becoming literate. To take advantage of the manner in which the Workbook was conceived, the educator must challenge those becoming educated to write what they want and what they can with the suggested words.

On page 7, in a little longer text, one returns to the question of practice:

Antonio, Maria, Pedro, and Fatima know how to read and write.
They learned to read by practicing reading.
They learned to write by practicing writing.
And by practicing one learns.

Let's write:

Once more, the blank space at the end serves as an invitation to those becoming literate to risk expressing themselves in writing. Throughout the Workbook, from the beginning to the end, those becoming literate are constantly challenged to write and read by practicing writing and reading. If it is impossible to write without practicing writing, then in a culture of predominantly oral memory such as São Tomé, a literacy program, respecting the culture as it is at the moment, needs both to stimulate the oral expression of those becoming literate — in debates, in the telling of stories, in the analysis of facts — and to challenge people to begin to write. To read and write are inseparable phases of the same process, representing the understanding and domination of the language and of language.

On page 11 a more complex but less extensive text is proposed that deals with aspects of colonial life and the present stage of national reconstruction. The text is preceded by some words that involve the central themes of national reconstruction.

The page begins like this:

Matabala is a kind of potato common in the São Tomé diet.

Let's read:
> School
> Plantation*
> Land
> To plant
> Product

Before Independence, the majority of our People did not have schools. The farms, with their lands for planting, belonged to the colonizers. The product of our work was theirs, too. Since Independence, everything is different. We have more schools for our children and the People began to study.

Let's write:

Still considering the oral nature of the culture in the state in which it is found, it is suggested to the facilitators that, not only in relation to this text but to all texts, they do a reading aloud first, slowly, which should be followed along silently by those becoming literate. Next, the learners should proceed in their silent reading for a certain time, after which they will begin to read aloud, one by one. Whatever the text may be, once the reading is finished, a discussion about it is indispensable.

In an effort to continue challenging those becoming literate to read critically and to write, at the same time that one proceeds to stimulate their oral expression, the following exercise is proposed to them on page 12:

> To practice always to learn
> > and
> to learn in order to practice better.

Let's read:
> Hoe
> Sowing
> Source
> Knowledge

Productive work is the source of knowledge. With the hoe we prepare the fields for sowing and we help to build a new country.
> Our children should learn by working
> Our schools should be schools of work.

Try to write about the text that you just read.
Write just as you speak. It is by practicing that one learns.

---

*A unit of production; for example, a cocoa plantation. Before independence there were altogether some seventy-five farms whose owners generally lived in Lisbon. The independent government's first action was to nationalize the farms.

If one studies the Exercise Workbook one notices how the challenge to the critical perception of those becoming literate gradually grows, page by page, along with the invitation for them to experience writing. If, however, the written word is foreign or almost foreign at a given moment of a culture, it is not such an easy task to introduce written language before or simultaneously to the infrastructural transformations that, in time, would come to demand it. At times, nevertheless, teaching written language is nondeferrable.

After some exercises that introduce the verbs *to be* and *to have* in the present indicative tense, but without any definition of what a verb is and any theoretical consideration relevant to their moods and tenses and personal inflections, one arrives at page 17, and one more challenge to the critical abilities of those becoming literate:

> We all know something. We are all ignorant of something.
> For this reason, we are always learning.*
>
> *Let's read, think, and discuss.*
> Working with perseverance, we produce more.
> Producing more, on the land that is ours, we create riches for the happiness of the people.
>
> With the MLSTP (Liberation Movement of São Tomé and Príncipe) we are building a society in which everyone participates for the well-being of all. We need to be watchful against those who are trying to bring back the system of exploitation of the majority by a dominant minority.
>
> Now try to write about what you read and discussed.

On pages 20 and 21 there are texts that exemplify the use of personal subject and object pronouns without making any allusion to grammatical principles. Page 20 reads:

> *Let's read.*
> I worry about our country. Carlos gave a book to Maria and another one to me. Two days later, Carlos came to the farm to speak with me.
>   I am your friend, I like you. Take this book I am giving you.
>   He wakes up early for work.

*Opposite page 16 is written: "No one is ignorant of everything. No one knows everything."

Sometimes he talks to himself, of himself, for himself.

She, too, talks to herself. They think about the future of their people at the same time that they work to make a future.

Every time I see him or her I talk to them about their studies.

I, me, to, for me, with me.

You, you, to you, of you, for you, with you.

He, she, himself, to himself, of himself, for himself, with himself, to him, him, her.

Write sentences with:
me, you, with me, to you, to me.

Page 21 reads:

Let's read.

We become independent at the cost of many sacrifices. With unity, discipline, and work we are consolidating our independence. We repel those who are against us and we gather together those who demonstrate their solidarity with us.

You, the colonialists, you were wrong to think that your power of exploitation was eternal. For you, it was impossible to believe that the weak, exploited masses would become a force in the struggle against your power.

You took with you almost everything that was ours, but you couldn't take with you our determined will to be free.

Maria, Julieta, Jorge, and Carlos — they struggled to increase production. They always bring with them the certainty of victory.

We, us, with us.

You, you, with you.

They, they, themselves, to themselves, of themselves, for themselves, with themselves, to them, them, them.

Write sentences with:
us, to them, with us.

On page 22 appears one of the many popular stories that, in cultures whose memory is still predominantly oral, pass from generation to generation and have an unquestionable pedagogical role. Part of the theoretical dimension of education in these cultures is realized through those stories, in which the use of metaphor is one of the riches of the popular language.

Popular education cannot be foreign to these stories, which reflect not only the dominant ideology but, mixed in with it, aspects of people's world views. In truth, these visions of the world are not a pure reproduction of that ideology. After reading the story on page 22, in which one recognizes, in written form, what one already knew through oral expression, a challenge is posed on page 23 to those becoming literate, so that they may write the following text, as well:

> You, comrade, can now do more than you did before. You can now write short stories. But before writing, think first about its practice. Think about the work next to the other comrades. Think about how they work the land, how they sow and how they harvest. Think about the instruments that they use on the farms or in the factories.
>
> If you, comrade, fish, think about the hours that you spend on the sea, on navigable waters, far from the beach, far from the lands of cultivation. Think about the stories of the fishermen. Think about the stories that you heard about the days of your grandparents. Afterward, try to write just as you speak. When you write the first story, you will see that you can write the second, the third, etc.
>
> It is by practicing that one learns.
>   Let's practice.
> Let's write your First Story.

On the following page it is suggested that those becoming literate write popular stories that will eventually fill whole anthologies. Look at the text:

> If you, comrades, write many stories, one day we will create a great book with stories told by our People. Stories that tell of our past, of the struggle of our People, of our resistance to the colonizer. Stories that tell of our traditions, our dances, music, parties. Stories that tell of the struggle today, of the national reconstruction. Stories that are pieces of our History..

Finally, the Exercise Workbook ends with the following text:

> You, comrades, have come to the end of this Exercise Workbook. And you have also come to the end of the First Popular Culture Notebook.
>
> By practicing reading and writing, you, comrades, learned to read and write at the same time that you discussed matters of interest to our People. You did not learn to read by memorizing by heart "ba-be-bi-bo-bu," by simply repeating "ta-te-ti-to-tu."

While you learned to read and write, you, comrades, discussed the national reconstruction, production, health, unity, discipline, and the work of our People in the national reconstruction. You conversed about the MLSTP, about its role in the vanguard of the People.

Now, together again, we are going to take a step forward in the search to know more, without ever forgetting that it is by practicing that one learns. Let's know better what we already know and know other things that we still do not know. All of us know something. All of us are ignorant of something. For this reason, we are always learning.

The search to know more continues in the struggle that continues.

Victory is ours.

Let us now see the
Second Popular Culture Notebook
  Our People
  Our Land
Texts to read and discuss
(Introduction to Grammar)

Before beginning the analysis, or more precisely the transcription of texts of this Notebook with commentary, it seems important to point out how practice altered the plans that we had in relation to the Exercise Workbook and the Second Popular Culture Notebook. While the former had been conceived as an aid to the person becoming literate, reinforcing the First Notebook in the literacy phase, the Second Notebook was thought of as the basic book of the first stage of postliteracy. In time it was perceived that this last role would fall to the Exercise Workbook, while the Second Notebook would come to be used on a more advanced level of postliteracy, along with the other Notebooks referred to at the bottom of page 4.[3] The Second Notebook begins with the following:

Introduction

With the First Popular Culture Notebook and the Exercise Workbook you learned to read in the practice of reading. You learned to write in the practice of writing. You practiced reading and writing at the same time that you also practiced discussing matters of interest to our People.

For us, it did not make sense to teach our People only b-a = ba. When we learn to read and write, it is also important to learn to think correctly. To think correctly we should think about our practice in work. We should think about our daily lives.

When we learn to read and write, it is important to try to better understand what colonial exploitation was, what our independence means, to better understand our struggle to create a fair society, without exploiters or exploited, a society of workers.

To learn to read to write is not to memorize "mouthfuls" of words in order to repeat them afterward.

With this Second Popular Culture Notebook you are going to be able to reinforce what you already know and to increase your knowledge, which is necessary for the struggle for national reconstruction. For this reason, you should try hard and work with discipline.

If you don't know the meaning of a word you find in the text, consult the vocabulary at the end of this Notebook. If the word you are looking for is not there, ask a comrade or talk to a cultural facilitator, who is your comrade, too.

The words with which the vocabulary is introduced are words of challenge, and not of accommodation:

In this vocabulary you will find the meaning of some words and groups of words that appear in the different texts of this Notebook. It is an aid that can serve you in your effort to comprehend the texts, which were written to be studied and not simply to be read, as if they were only "reading lessons." The vocabulary alone does not resolve your difficulties. You have to work to understand the vocabulary.

It is not by chance that the first theme dealt with in the Second Popular Culture Notebook is the act of studying. It is presented in two parts, as is the case with the majority of the themes, though some are discussed in three parts. It seemed necessary to begin this Notebook by provoking a debate on the act of studying, whose meaning could be learned from the relating of a simple story.

The Act of Studying: I

It had rained all night. There were enormous pools of water in the lowest parts of the land. In certain places, the earth was so soaked that it had turned into mud. At times, one's feet slid on it. At times, rather than sliding, one's feet became stuck in the mud up to the ankles. It was difficult to walk. Pedro and Antonio were transporting baskets full of cocoa beans in a truck to the place where they were to be dried. At a certain point the truck could not cross a mudhole in front of them. They stopped. They got out of the truck. They looked at the mudhole; it was a problem for them. They crossed two meters of mud, protected by their high-legged boots. They felt the thickness of the mud. They thought about it. They discussed how to resolve the problem. Then, with the help of some rocks and dry tree branches, they established the minimal consistency in the dirt for the wheels of the truck to pass over it without getting stuck.

Pedro and Antonio studied. They tried to understand the problem they had to resolve and, immediately, they found an answer. One does not study only in school.

Pedro and Antonio studied while they worked. To study is to assume a serious and curious attitude in the face of a problem.

The Act of Studying: II

This curious and serious attitude in the search to understand things and facts characterizes the act of studying. It doesn't matter that study is done at the time and in the place of our work, as in the case of Pedro and Antonio, which we just saw. It doesn't matter that study is done in another place and another time, like the study that we did in the Culture Circle. Study always demands a serious and curious attitude in the search to understand the things and facts we observe.

A text to be read is a text to be studied. A text to be studied is a text to be interpreted. We cannot interpret a text if we read it without paying attention, without curiosity; if we stop reading at the first difficulty. What would have become of the crop of cocoa beans on that farm if Pedro and Antonio had stopped carrying on the work because of a mudhole?

If a text is difficult, you insist on understanding it. You work with it as Antonio and Pedro did in relation to the problem of the mudhole.

To study demands discipline. To study is not easy, because to study is to create and re-create and not to repeat what others say.

To study is a revolutionary duty!

The preoccupation of this text with the act of studying seems obvious; for example, combating the ideological, though not always explicit, belief that one only studies in school. School may be considered, from this point of view, *the* matrix of knowledge. Outside of academia there is no knowledge, or the knowledge that exists is believed to be inferior, to have nothing to do with the rigorous knowledge of the intellectual. In truth, however, this disdained knowledge, "knowledge made from experience," has to be the point of departure in any popular educational effort oriented toward the creation of a more rigorous knowledge on the part of the people. While an expression of the dominant ideology, this myth about academia deeply influences the people, sometimes provoking disdain for themselves due to their feeling that they have little or no "reading."[4]

It becomes necessary, then, to emphasize practical activity in concrete reality (activity that never lacks a technical intellectual dimension,[5] however simple it may be) as a generator of knowledge. The act of studying social as well as individual character functions independently of its subjects' awareness of it. Basically, the act of studying, a curious act of the subject facing the world, is an expression of a form of existing. Since human beings are social, historical beings, they are doers, they are transformers, they not only know, but they know that they know.

It is also necessary to point out that this curiosity about the object or fact under observation, while demanding an understanding of the object (which should not be described only according to its appearance), leads us to search for the reason for the existence of the object or fact.

Another preoccupation that one finds in this text on the act of studying, one that is present throughout the Notebook, is the reference to the people's right to know better what they already know. This is to facilitate their practice (to bring about a more rigorous understanding of the facts partially learned and explained), so that they can know what they still don't know. In this process, one counts on the ability of the popular masses to do, to think, to know, and to create. One does not particularly deal with delivering or transferring to the people more rigorous explanations of the facts, as though these facts were finalized, rigid, and ready to be digested. One is concerned with stimulating and challenging them.

As Antonio Gramsci commented:

> One is persuaded that a truth is fertile only when an effort has been made to conquer it. That it does not exist in itself and for itself, but results from a conquest of the spirit. Similarly, in each individual it is necessary to reproduce that state of anxiety that the studious person has crossed before reaching [a truth]. This

representation is much more educational than the schematic exposition of this same knowledge to the hearer of efforts, errors, and gradual dexterity through which men have passed to reach actual knowledge. Teaching, developed in this way, becomes an act of liberation.[6]

The next theme dealt with in the Second Popular Culture Notebook is:

National Reconstruction: I

The national reconstruction is the effort in which our People are engaged to create a new society. A society of workers. But, notice, if we said that we have to create a new society it is because it does not happen by accident. For this reason, the national reconstruction is a struggle that continues.

To produce more on the farms and in the factories, to work more in the public services, and to struggle for the national reconstruction; no one in São Tomé and Príncipe has the right to fold his arms and expect others to do things for him. Without production on the farms and in the factories, without work dedicated to public service, we will not create the new society.

National Reconstruction: II

We saw, in the previous text, that to produce more on the farms, in the factories, and to work more in the public services is to struggle for national reconstruction. We also saw that, for us, national reconstruction means the creation of a new society, without exploited or exploiters. A society of workers. For this reason, the national reconstruction demands of us:

Unity
Discipline
Work
Vigilance

- *Unity* of all, having the same objective in sight: *the creation of a new society.*
- *Discipline* in action, in work, in study, in daily life. Conscious discipline, without which nothing is done, nothing created. Discipline in unity, without which work is lost.
- *Work.* Work on the farms. Work in the factories. Work in public service. Work in schools.
- *Vigilance*, much vigilance, against the internal and external enemies, who will do anything they can to deter our struggle for the creation of the new society.

This text, as simple as it was, posed the problem of the national reconstruction and played with the words *unity, discipline, work,* and *vigilance.* Obviously, the theme of the national reconstruction or the reinvention of the society of São Tomé is imposed by its present state. The game played with the words *unity, discipline, work,* and *vigilance,* which appear in a great number of slogans, was introduced to present them in a dynamic text preserving or recovering their most profound meaning (threatened by the uncritical character of clichés).

Clearly, it has been my intention in the second part of this chapter to excerpt those texts of the Second Popular Culture Notebook that are in consonance with the points I made in the first part. Here is one more such text:

Work and Transformation of the World: I

Pedro and Antonio cut down a tree. They had practice doing it. The practical activity of human beings has objectives. They knew what they wanted to do when they cut down the tree. They had worked. With instruments, they not only cut down the tree but they trimmed it after cutting it down. They divided the large trunk into pieces, which they dried in the sun. Immediately afterward, Pedro and Antonio sawed the pieces of the trunk and made boards with them. With the boards, they made a boat. Before making the boat, even before they cut down the tree, they had already conceived in their heads the form of the boat that they were going to make. They already knew their reason for making the boat. Pedro and Antonio worked. They transformed the tree with their work and made a boat with it. It is by working that men and women transform the world, and by transforming the world, they transform themselves, too.

Work and Transformation of the World: II

Pedro and Antonio made the boat with the boards. They made the boards with the pieces of the large trunk that they cut down. When the big tree was divided into pieces, it stopped being a tree. When the pieces of the trunk became boards, they stopped being pieces of the trunk. When Pedro and Antonio constructed the boat with boards, the boards stopped being boards. They became a boat.

The tree belongs to the world of nature. The boat, made by Antonio and Pedro, belongs to the world of culture, since it is the world that human beings make with their creative work.

The boat is culture.

The way to use the boat is culture.

Dance is culture.

Work and Transformation of the World: III

Work that transforms does not always dignify men and women. Only free work gives us courage. The only work that dignifies us is that by which we contribute to the creation of a just society, without exploiters or exploited.

In the colonial days, our work was not free. We worked for the interests of the colonialists, who exploited us. They took over our lands and our work force and became rich at our expense. The richer they became, the poorer we became. They were the exploiting minority. We were the exploited majority. Today, we are independent. We no longer work for a minority. We work to create a fair society. We still have much to do.[7]

Regarding an introduction to grammar, a simple but fairly complete study of verbs was done, supporting the texts presented up to this point.

The Struggle for Liberation: I

The MLSTP guided the struggle for the liberation of our People.

The PAIGC guided the struggle for the liberation of the People of Guinea and Cape Verde.

The MPLA, the Workers Party, guided the struggle for the Liberation of the Angolan People.

The FRELIMO guided the struggle for the liberation of the People of Mozambique.*

The independence of all of us, People of São Tomé and Príncipe, Guineans, Cape Verdians, Angolans, and Mozambicans, was not a gift from the colonialists. Our independence resulted from a hard and difficult struggle. A struggle in which all of us participated, as oppressed People, seeking liberation. Each one of these populations united in the struggle in which they were able to fight, and the sum of their struggles overthrew the colonialists.

Our struggle in Africa was decisive for the victory of the Portuguese People against the dictatorship that dominated them. Without our struggle, April 25 in Portugal would not have been realized.

But our struggle was not made against any race or against the Portuguese People. We struggled against the system of colonialist exploration, against imperialism, against all forms of exploitation.

---

*PAIGC stands for African Party for the Independence of Guinea and Cape Verde. (The attempt at unity between Guinea and Cape Verde, suggested by the name of the party, ended in November 1980 with the political change that came to Guinea-Bissau.) MPLA stands for Movement for the Liberation of Angola. FRELIMO stands for Liberation Front of Mozambique.

The national reconstruction is the continuation of this struggle, for the creation of a just society.

An important point upon which to constantly reflect in discussing the struggle for liberation and national reconstruction is that the people are the subjects of their history too. Their political presence and their voice in the process of reconstruction are what I made reference to in the first part of this chapter.

The Struggle for Liberation: II

The sacrifice of our struggle against colonialism would be useless if our independence meant only the replacement of the colonialists by a privileged national minority. If this were so, our People would continue to be exploited by the dominant classes of the imperialist countries by means of the national minority. For this reason, national reconstruction means for us the creation of a new society, a society of workers, without exploiters or exploited.

Let's not leave for tomorrow what we can do today.
The Struggle continues!

A new society, a new man, a new woman, all these were — and continue to be — expressions incorporated into the language of revolutionary transition. It seemed, and continues to seem, important to call attention to the fact that the generation of the new society — like that of the new man and the new woman — does not result from a mechanical act. The new society is delivered through birth; it does not appear by decree or automatically.

And birth, which is a process, is always more difficult than it seems.

The New Society

What is a new society without exploiters or the exploited? It is a society in which no man, no woman, no group of people, no class exploits the work force of others. It is a society in which there are no privileges for those who work with the pen and only obligations for those who work with their hands on the farms and in the factories. All workers are to serve in the well-being of everyone.

A society like this is not created overnight. But it is necessary for the people to begin to have the idea in their heads of this form of society today, as Pedro and Antonio had in their heads the form of the boat that they were going to make before they cut down the tree.

Do you remember how Pedro and Antonio made the boat? They cut down a tree. They trimmed the tree. They cut its trunk into pieces. With the pieces they made boards and with the boards they made the boat. But even before they cut down the tree, Pedro and Antonio already had in their heads the form of the boat that they were going to make and already knew why they were going to make the boat. Pedro and Antonio worked; they transformed nature.

To make the new society, we, too, need to work, we need to transform the old society we still have. It is easier, without a doubt, to make a boat than to create a new society. But if Pedro and Antonio made the boat, the People of São Tomé and Príncipe, with unity, discipline, work, and vigilance, will create a new society with its vanguard, the MLSTP.

In the next text it is again stated that there is no ignorance that is absolute, and that the people have the right to know better what they already know and to know what they still do not know.

No One Is Ignorant of Everything. No One Knows Everything.

No one is ignorant of everything. No one knows everything. We all know something. We are all ignorant of something.

Pedro, for example, knows how to gather cocoa very well. He learned from practice as a child how to gather the cocoa bean without ruining the tree. He need only look to know if the bean is ready to be harvested. But Pedro does not know how to print a newspaper. Antonio learned from very early on through practice how one must work to print a newspaper, but he doesn't know how to harvest cocoa. Harvesting cocoa and printing a newspaper are practices equally necessary to the national reconstruction.

The knowledge that Pedro gained from the practice of harvesting cocoa is not enough. Pedro needs to know more. The same thing can be said of Antonio. The knowledge that Antonio gained from the practice of printing the newspaper is not enough. Antonio needs to know more. Antonio has the right to know more. Antonio can know more. To study to serve the People is not only a right but also a revolutionary duty. Let's study!

Manual Work—Intellectual Work

Men and women work, that is, they act and think. They work because they do much more than the horse that pulls the plow to serve man. They work because they are capable of foreseeing, programming, and finding objectives for the work itself. In work, the human being uses his whole body. He uses his hands and his ability to think. The human body is a conscious body. For that reason, it is wrong to separate so-called manual labor from so-called intellectual work. The factory workers and the farm workers are intellectuals too. Only in societies in which using one's hands in practical activities is scorned are harvesting cocoa or printing newspapers considered inferior.

In the society that we are creating, we do not separate manual from intellectual activity. For this reason, our schools will be schools of work. Our children will learn, from very early on, by working. The day will come when, in São Tomé and Príncipe, no one will work in order to study, nor will anyone study in order to work — because all will study when working.

Practice Teaches Us

We cannot deny that practice teaches us. We cannot deny that we know many things because of practice. We cannot deny, for example, that we know if it is going to rain when we look at the sky and see the clouds are a certain color. We even know if it will be light rain or a storm.

From the time we were young we learned to understand the world that surrounds us. Thus, even before learning to read and write words and sentences, we are already "reading," well or poorly, the world that surrounds us. But the knowledge we gain from practice is not enough. We could make another Notebook dealing with the matters that you, comrades, have suggested to us.

To study is a revolutionary duty!

The Productive Process: I

The wood for the boards with which doors, windows, tables, and boats are made is found, in its natural state, in the trees in the forests. The steel to make hammers, hoes, and scythes is found, in its natural state, under the land. Human beings, through work, transform *natural materials*, making from them *raw materials*. Natural materials (like the already-worked iron and the already-prepared wood) are called *objects of work*.

The land to be prepared for the cultivation of rice is an object of work.

The trees to be cut down, from which boards may be made, are objects of work.

The boards to be transformed into tables, chairs, doors, and windows are objects of work.

The Productive Process: II

To transform natural materials into raw materials and to produce something with raw materials, we need instruments. We need machines, tools, and transportation. These things we need to help us produce — that is, the instruments, the tools, the machines, and the transportation — are called the *means of work*.

Natural materials, raw materials, and the means of work combine to form the *means of production*.

The following are means of production on a farm:

- lands for cultivation
- natural materials
- raw materials
- instruments, the tools, the transportation.

The Productive Process: III

We already saw that if there was no human work, the tree would not be transformed into boards, nor would the iron, in its natural state, become sheets of metal. All this is done because of human work, because of the work force.

The means of production and the workers constitute what is called the productive forces of a society.

Production results from the combination of the means of production and the work force. In order to understand a society it is important to know in what way its productive process is organized. It is necessary to know how the means of production and the work force combine. It is necessary to know the nature of the social relations that come into play in production: if they are relations of exploitation or relations of equality and collaboration between everyone.

In the colonial period, the social relations of production were those of exploitation. Thus, they were violent. The colonialists took power over the means of production and our work force. They were absolute owners of the land, of the natural materials, of the raw materials, of the tools, the machines, the transportation, and the work force. Nothing escaped their power and control.

When we speak today about national reconstruction to create a new society, we are talking about a really different society, a society in which the social relations of production will no longer be those of exploitation, but of equality and collaboration between everyone.

The following text again discusses the nonmechanic nature of the social transformation.

The Action of Transforming

We are in this room. Here a Culture Circle is at work. The room is organized in a certain way. The chairs, the table, the blackboard — all occupy a certain place in the room. There are posters on the walls, figures, designs. It would not be difficult for us to organize the room in a different way. If we felt the need to do this, in a short time, together, we would change the positions of the chairs, the table, the blackboard, completely. The reorganization of the room, according to the newly recognized needs, would demand from us a little physical effort and work as a group. In this way, we would transform the old organization of the room and create a new one, according to other objectives.

To reorganize the old society, to transform it to create the new society, is not as easy as this. For this reason, the new society is not created overnight, nor does the new society appear by chance. It only happens when there are profound transformations in the old society.

The two texts that follow deal with the problem of culture and cultural identity, themes of the highest importance, especially in a society that is still somewhat colonial.

People and Culture

The colonialists used to say that only they had culture. They said that before their arrival in Africa we did not have a History. That our History began with their coming. These statements are false. They were necessary to the despoiling practice that the colonialists exercised over us. To prolong our economic exploitation as long as possible, they needed to attempt the destruction of our cultural identity, deny our culture, our History.

All People have culture, because they work, because they transform the world, and upon transforming it, they are transformed.

The dance of the People is culture.

The music of the People is culture, as is the way in which the People cultivate the land. Culture is also the way in which the People walk, smile, talk, and sing, while they work.

The calulu* is culture, as is the way of making calulu, as is our taste for foods. Culture is made of the instruments that People use to produce. Culture is the way in which the People understand and express their world and how the People understand themselves in their relation to their world. Culture is the beat of the drum that sounds in the night. Culture is the beat of the

*A dish made with palm oil. It can be prepared with chicken, fish, or beef.

drum. Culture is the swaying of the bodies of the People to the beat of the drums.

The Defense of Our Culture

One of the preoccupations of our Movement and our Government is the defense of our culture. For this reason, President Pinto da Costa said: "Upon liquidating the colonial culture, we have to create in our country a new culture, based on our traditions. This new culture that we will create in our country will take advantage of the positive aspects of our traditions, banishing all their negative aspects. Naturally, the new culture should not close the doors to the positive influences of foreign cultures. It will be open to the culture of all the other populations, but will always preserve our national character."

For this reason, we need to produce, we need to create and re-create. We need to study without becoming dispirited. We need to develop a science and a technique. We cannot stop at the first obstacle that we meet.

The preoccupation with a critical form of thinking is again manifested in the following two texts.

Thinking Correctly: I

Our principal objective in writing the texts of this Notebook is to challenge you, comrades, to think correctly. What do we mean by challenging you to think correctly? *To challenge* is a verb that means not only to call to battle, but also to pose a problem, that is, to question, stimulate, provoke.[8]

Just as in literacy efforts it does not interest us to teach the People "b-a = ba," it also does not interest us, in post literacy, to give the People sentences and texts to read without understanding them. The national reconstruction demands from all of us conscious participation, at any level of the national reconstruction, demands action and thought, practice and theory. There is no practice without theory, no theory without practice.

To think correctly means to try to discover and understand what is found to be hidden away in things and in facts that we observe and analyze. To discover, for example, that it is not "being poorly regarded" that makes little Pedro sad, but rather that he has worms.

Therefore, we will bring happiness to little Pedro not through incantations, but through medical guidance.

Return, now, to the previous texts of your Notebook. At home, when you have some free time, read one and then another. Think hard about each line, about each statement, and try to understand better what you have read.

To Think Correctly: II

To think correctly, to discover the reason for the existence of facts, and to make the knowledge that practice gives us more profound are not the privileges of a few, but a right that the People have in a revolutionary society. Our Government, in agreement with the political orientation of our Movement, is trying to attend to this right of our People. In addition to re-orientation of the way of producing and the stimulus to production, our Government is worried about the systematic education of the People.

Now try to do an exercise, attempting to think correctly. Write on a piece of paper how you see this problem: "Can the education of children and adults, after the Independence of our country, be equal to the education that we had before Independence?"

If you think that it can be the same, say why.

If you think that it cannot be, say why.

If, for you, the present education should be different from the education that we had before Independence, point out some aspects of this difference.

Before offering any more excerpts from the Notebook, let's consider one or two points in the field of study of the language specifically, and of language in general.

In the Notebook, the introduction to grammar does not go beyond an analysis of the so-called grammatical categories. The introduction is never, however, done in a formal or mechanical way. On the contrary, it is always dynamic.

One need of the participants of the circles of postliteracy is to be able to read documents of the Movement, official documents of the Government, and the newspaper *Revolution*. One of our solutions has been to introduce the use of the relative pronoun *que* (that or which). This pronoun is used in sentences very common in popular discourse, though it is sometimes abused. The more these sentences distance the subject from its verb, the more difficult it is to understand the discourse. In truth, popular groups don't speak. In view of this, one should equip the popular groups so they have command of this form of language, which reveals another structure of thinking that is not their own.

On page 51 of the Notebook it says:

Among other types of pronouns, we are now going to learn one more, a very important one. But we are going to become familiar with it through examples.

The book that I bought is good.

Observe: before the word *that*, we have the word *book*.

Book, as you know, is a masculine, singular, common noun.

If you now substitute the word *that* for *which*, you will see that the meaning of the thought is the same. It doesn't matter whether you say the book that I bought is good or the book which I bought is good.

Another example:

The farm that I visited is beautiful.

In this example, before the word *that* we have the word *farm*.

Farm, as you know, is a common, feminine, singular noun. If you now substitute the word *that*, which comes after farm, with *which*, you will see that the meaning of the thought is the same. It doesn't matter whether you say "The farm that I visited is beautiful" or "The farm which I visited is beautiful."

Pay attention: each time the word *that* can be substituted by the masculine, feminine, masculine plural, or feminine plural form of *which*, the word *that* is a pronoun.

Other examples:

The text that I read is good.

I understood the pages that you wrote.

The farm that produces more is this one.

On page 53 of the Notebook:

Let's learn to use the word *whose*, another very important pronoun.

1. The child whose father arrived from Angola is this one.

2. I came from a farm whose cocoa production this year is very high.

3. The Culture Circle whose participants worked more received a congratulatory letter from the Comrade President.

4. We work seriously on the reading of this book whose pages that were more difficult received profound attention.

In the first example, *whose* is equal to *of which*.

Observe how substituting *whose* for *of which* does not alter the meaning of the sentence:

The child whose father arrived from Angola is this one.

In the second example, *whose* (feminine) is equal to *of which* (feminine), because of the feminine noun *farm*, which precedes it:

I came from a farm whose production...

In the third example, *whose* (masculine plural), is equal to *of which*, because of the Culture Circle:

The Culture Circle whose participants worked more.

In the fourth example, *whose*, (feminine plural) is equal to *of which*, because of *book*:

We worked seriously on the reading of this book whose pages. . . .

Now, a series of examples constituting adjectival sentences with the pronoun *that*.

Here we have two groups of words with complete meaning:

I bought this book today. It is good.

The first group of words is:

I bought this book today.

The second group of words is:

It is good.

Now, by organizing these groups of words in a different way, we can say the same thing that we said before. For this effect, we are going to use the pronoun, *that*, which we just learned:

This book that I bought today is good.

Another example:

These men participated actively in the voluntary work.

They just arrived very happily from the farm.

Again, we have two groups of words.

The first group:

These men participated actively in the voluntary work.

The second group:

They just arrived happily from the farm.

Let us now see how we can say the same thing with the pronoun *who*:

These men, who participated actively in the voluntary work, just arrived happily from the farm.

One more example:

The comrades defended themselves against tetanus. The comrades were vaccinated against it .

The first group of words:

The comrades defended themselves against tetanus.

The second group of words:

The comrades were vaccinated against it.

Now with the pronoun *who*:

The comrades, who defended themselves against tetanus, were vaccinated against it.

Let us now see the last texts, which, together with those that appeared earlier, give us a general view of the Notebook:

The Evaluation of Practice

It is impossible to practice without evaluating practice. To evaluate practice is to analyze what one does, comparing the results obtained with the objectives we tried to reach with practice. The evaluation of practice reveals judgments, errors, and imprecisions. Evaluation corrects practice, betters practice, and increases our efficiency. The work of evaluating practice never stops being a part of it.

You, comrades, have a practice in this Culture Circle. You work with the cultural facilitator, you follow a program with views oriented toward certain objectives. You are in the Culture Circle and are involved in the practice of reading better and better, of interpreting what you read, of writing, of communicating, of increasing the knowledge that you already have and of learning what you still do not know. The national reconstruction needs our People to know our reality more and better. Our People need to prepare themselves to present a solution to our problems. The Coordinating Commission of the Popular Culture Circles is the sector of the Ministry of Education in charge of organizing, preparing, planning, and executing a part of our educational policy. It develops all this, with the adults, in the Culture Circles. The Coordinating Commission, then, cannot stop evaluating the practice that is performed in these Circles. But you, comrades, should also evaluate your own practice. You should constantly examine the advances you are making and try to overcome the difficulties you encounter. If you, comrades, analyze your own practice, you will be participating with the comrade facilitator and the Coordinating Commission in search of better instruments of work.

Practice needs evaluation
like fish need water
and farming needs rain.

Planning of Practice

We already saw that there is no practice without evaluation. But practice demands its planning, too. To plan practice means to have a clear idea of the objectives we want to reach with it. It means to have a knowledge of the conditions in which we are going to act, of the instruments and of the means that are available to us. To plan practice also means to know whom we can count on to carry it out. To plan means to foresee deadlines, the different moments of action that should be evaluated continuously. We can plan for the short term, the middle term, and the long term. Sometimes evaluation teaches us that, even if the objectives that we had were correct, the means that we chose were not the best. Sometimes we also perceive that, through the practice of evaluation, the deadlines that we had determined did not correspond to our real possibilities.

All the activities of our country need to be planned and executed better.

What would become of our economy if we were not prepared to harvest the cocoa when it was ready? The cocoa beans would perish and it would be a disaster for everyone. It is important that our People understand the need to evaluate their practice and the need to participate in the plans for national reconstruction.

The New Man and the New Woman

The new man and the new woman do not appear by accident. The new man and the new woman are born in the practice of the revolutionary reconstruction of the society.

Let's think about some qualities that characterize the new man and the new woman. One of these qualities is agreement with the People's cause and the defense of the People's interests. Fulfilling our duty, no matter what task falls to us, is a sign of the new man and the new woman. The correct sense of political militancy, in which we are learning to overcome individualism and egoism, is also a sign of the new man and the new woman. The intolerant defense of our autonomy, of the freedom we fought for, also marks the new man and the new woman. The sense of solidarity, not only with our People, but also with all of the People who struggle for their liberation, is another characteristic of the new man and the new woman. Not to leave for tomorrow what you can do today, and to do what you should do better each day — these are proper qualities of the new man and the new woman. To participate, consciously, in the efforts of national reconstruction is a duty of the new man and the new woman.

To study (a revolutionary duty), to think correctly, to develop curiosity in the face of reality, to create and re-create, to criticize with justice and to accept constructive criticism, to combat antipopular activities — all these are characteristics of the new man and the new woman.

By participating more and more in the struggle for national reconstruction, we are letting the new man and the new woman be born in ourselves.

The New Man, the New Woman, and Education

One of the most important qualities of the new man and the new woman is the certainty that one cannot stop marching, that soon the new will become old if it is not renewed. The education of children, young adults, and adults has great importance in the education of the new man and the new woman. It has to be a new education, as well, that we are trying to put into practice according to our possibilities. A completely different education from that of colonial days. An education through work, which stimulates collaboration, not competition. An education that places value on mutual help, not on individualism; that develops a critical spirit and creativity, not passivity. An education that is based on the unity between practice and theory, between manual labor and intellectual work, and for this reason motivates those becoming educated to think correctly.

It has to be an education that does not favor lies, false ideas, or lack of discipline. It has to be political education, as political as any other education, but one that does not try to be neutral. Upon declaring that it is not neutral — that neutrality is, indeed, impossible — the new education affirms that its policy is that of the interests of our People.

With the following text, which closes the Notebook, I can also conclude this chapter.

Comrade,

You have come to the end of the Second Popular Culture Notebook. We hope that you have enjoyed the experience it offered to you. We hope you enjoyed the experience of increasing the knowledge that you already had through your practice, even before you began to read and write; the experience of consolidating and making more profound, as a part of a group, the knowledge that you obtained in the first phase of your studies, as well as the knowledge of gaining further knowledge. We hope you enjoyed the experience of discussing in a more organized manner a great number and variety of themes, starting with the reading of texts. But above all, we hope that you have perceived that our revolutionary task could not be that of simply giving information. Our revolutionary task demands that we not only inform correctly but also educate. One does not really become educated if one does not assume responsibilities in the act of becoming educated. Our People will not become educated through passivity, but through action, and always in unity with thought. Thus our preoccupation with challenging you, comrades, to think, to analyze reality. This is the orientation that characterizes all the Popular Culture Notebooks that you, comrades, are getting to know, and that you will come to know.

5

Literacy in Guinea-Bissau Revisited

Macedo: Why did you become interested and, later, involved in the illiteracy problem in Guinea-Bissau?

Freire: Let me begin by saying that even before my interest in the literacy campaign in Guinea-Bissau, I was extremely interested in the struggle for liberation of the African people in general. With great curiosity and even greater happiness, I closely followed the struggle of liberation in Mozambique, Angola, Cape Verde, São Tomé and Príncipe, and Guinea-Bissau, keeping in mind the distinct nature of these struggles. The differences in these struggles were conditioned obviously by the different historical and geographical contexts. Even before the independence of Guinea-Bissau, then, I already had an attachment — both political and affective to that country and its heroic people.

It was precisely these cultural, political, and affective links with Africa that fueled my interest in the literacy campaign in Guinea-Bissau. As a man from northeastern Brazil, I was somewhat culturally tied to Africa, particularly to those countries that were unfortunate enough to be colonized by Portugal, as was Brazil.

In 1970 or 1971, I made my first trip to Africa, to Tanzania and Zambia. After my arrival in Zambia, while I was waiting at the airport for a domestic flight to take me to my final destination, where I was to work with an educational team, I was paged and asked to report to the information counter. There I was met by a North American couple who represented MPLA (the Popular Movement for the Liberation of Angola), a group that included Lara, an important political figure not only in Angola but also throughout all of Africa.

The North American couple came with a proposal from the leaders of the MPLA, asking me if I would change my flight so I could spend a day meeting with some representatives of the MPLA who were most interested in talking to me. I immediately accepted. I looked forward to meeting with a group whose work for the freedom of their people I had admired and closely followed. We went to the North Americans' house where Lara, along with five more MPLA militants, was waiting.

Lara greeted me by saying: "Comrade Paulo Freire, if you knew my country as well as we know your work, you would know Angola extremely well!" We talked most of the afternoon about the ongoing struggle (at that time the fight for liberation in Angola was experiencing some setbacks) and, most important, we discussed at great length the role of literacy work in the struggle for liberation. We also discussed the literacy difficulties in Mozambique and Guinea-Bissau.

(Incidentally, the World Council of Churches, where I worked, had lent strong support to many African liberation movements even before my participation. I was not the one who initiated the involvement of the World Council with these movements. What I did was try to reinforce the already existing relationships.)

In addition to political and military concerns of the moment, Lara and I analyzed the nature of the new educational process taking place during the struggle, particularly in the areas that were being liberated. We discussed the practice of the struggle as a pedagogical praxis. At night, after supper, the MPLA members showed me documentary films about the liberation struggle and the pedagogical experience taking place during the struggle. This encounter with African liberation leaders preceded my involvement, and that of the team of educators I worked with, in Guinea-Bissau. In certain respects, it prepared me for what would later become our educational contribution to both Guinea-Bissau and Angola.

After Zambia, I went to Tanzania. I witnessed many of the same things there as in Zambia. At the University of Tanzania I was approached by a Tanzanian who was deeply involved with FRELIMO (the Liberation Front of Mozambique). He asked me if I would accept an invitation to meet with representatives of FRELIMO in Dar Es Salaam. I accepted. Among those present was the widow of Mondlame, the assassinated leader of FRE-LIMO. The present minister of education of Mozambique was also there. As in Zambia with the MPLA, we had conversations about education, its role and processes during the struggle for liberation.

I was then invited to visit the training camp that the president of Tanzania had set up for the FRELIMO fighters. Intensive training was preparing literacy teachers, who would later go into Mozambique to work in the literacy campaigns under way at the same time as the war for liberation. An important highlight of this training was the emphasis on not dichotomizing the struggles for freedom and literacy. In the training camp I met with educational leaders, including many Europeans committed to the Liberation struggle who were there to help.

I was happy to see that what was important for the European and African youths was the ideological strength informing the struggle to restore self-respect and dignity, which had been usurped by a cruel and vicious colonial machinery. It was clear to me that these European youths were on the side of the popular masses from Mozambique, who were fighting for their freedom. During that meeting we discussed the techniques and literacy methods they were using.

Then, in January 1975, while in Geneva, I received a long letter from Jose Maria Nunes Pereira, a Brazilian professor from the Catholic University of Rio de Janeiro, who was then serving as coordinator of African and Asian Studies at Candido Mendes University, also in Rio de Janeiro. Professor Pereira wrote that as coordinator of Africa and Asian Studies, he had recently returned from Guinea-Bissau, where he had had a long meeting with the minister of education, Mario Cabral, and with the president of Guinea-Bissau, Luis Cabral, brother of Amilcar Cabral, the founder of PAIGC. In his letter, Pereira stressed that both the president and minister of education had urged him to ask me if I would accept an invitation to coordinate a team of educators in the literacy campaign in Guinea-Bissau. This campaign focused on adult literacy, but it also included other areas of education. If I was interested, I was to contact Mario Cabral.

After I received Pereira's letter, I organized a meeting at my house with other members of IDAC (Institute for Cultural Action) to discuss the letter and the possibility of establishing a collaborative program with Guinea-Bissau. Everybody from IDAC showed great interest in helping the Guinea-Bissau program. The next day I also discussed the invitation with the World Council of Churches. My intentions were to devise a plan in which the World Council and IDAC would work together, studying and planning ways to best contribute and meet the challenges of eradicating illiteracy in Guinea-Bissau. Both IDAC and the World Council accepted my proposal, and that January I wrote Mario Cabral. The first few lines of that letter mentioned that I received a letter from someone who had been in Guinea-Bissau. Why did I not mention Professor Pereira's name in this letter? At the time, Brazil had in place an extremely repressive political machine. My own exile taught me to be careful about citing names because under the Brazilian dictatorship, I might endanger people's positions, or even their lives.

Continuing, I wrote: "The individual who wrote me from Brazil has discussed with you and the president the possibility of organizing a team of educators in which I would contribute to the adult literacy program already in place in Guinea-Bissau. He further suggested that I write you to begin a conversation on how to get started."

In April 1975, two and a half months after I wrote Mario Cabral, he answered my letter. That April I wrote him a second letter, which begins:

"Dear Comrade Mario Cabral: I just received your letter, in which you confirm the government's interest in our collaboration. I do not think it necessary to expand on our satisfaction in receiving this confirmation, satisfaction not only on the part of members of IDAC but also of the World Council of Churches."

In this second letter I proposed some guidelines, including

the possibility of sending someone to Geneva to begin discussion on the general educational situation of Guinea-Bissau. We had proposed that Mario Cabral come to Geneva. I realize now that he was probably too busy to accept our invitation.

Macedo: Did you and your team of educators support your own educational activities in Guinea-Bissau?

Paulo: In responding to this question, I can put to rest some small-minded criticism some have harbored against me. Some have said I offered huge grants to Guinea-Bissau and bought my way through Guinea-Bissau. In other words, Guinea-Bissau was not really interested in our contribution to the literacy campaign, but could not refuse the money. This type of criticism not only offends those of us who genuinely wanted to contribute to the reconstruction of the educational system, but also those comrades who fought heroically in the jungles of Guinea-Bissau to defeat the colonialists. It would be unlikely that they would fight for twelve years only to sell their interests so easily in the face of some small offer of financial support that we could have made. But let us put this type of criticism aside and try to answer your question.

As I said earlier, the World Council of Churches played an important role in the movements for liberation in Africa. The World Council never ceased to give assistance to those liberation movements, even in difficult times during their struggles. The World Council also saw to it that the contributions it gave during these struggles would continue during the reconstruction of the new societies after independence from colonial powers. It was certainly not inappropriate that the World Council raised about $500,000 to assist the literacy campaign in Nicaragua, for instance. I was part of a team of educators who took part in this campaign in Nicaragua.

But the World Council did not limit its assistance to Nicaragua and Guinea-Bissau. It also offered a tremendous amount of help in Angola, Mozambique, and other countries. So when the department where I worked at the World Council had the opportunity to contribute to Guinea-Bissau, and made a commitment to provide technical assistance, it also accepted the financial commitment that went along with it. That is, even though the department had little money, it paid my salary while I was in

Guinea-Bissau, as if I had been in Geneva. The same procedure applied with respect to my trips to Angola, São Tomé, and Cape Verde. But the CCPD, a sector of the World Council that dealt with educational and developmental programs, had the financial means to support certain educational projects and programs in the Third World. The CCPD was interested in the project in Guinea-Bissau, and IDAC presented a proposal seeking financial support from CCPD.

When I first went to Guinea-Bissau, my travel expenses were paid by the World Council. The rest of the team that accompanied me was financed by CCPD. After I received Pereira's letter, I wrote Mario Cabral in Guinea-Bissau saying that I would accept his invitation to put together a team of educators to work there in adult literacy, but that the government did not have to pay the travel expenses, salaries, and other costs that the group would incur. Given the economic conditions of the recently independent Guinea-Bissau, we knew this would have been impossible. By agreeing to provide technical assistance to the literacy campaign, we wanted to try, as much as we could, not to burden financially an already economically depressed country. So it was arranged that the IDAC team going to Guinea-Bissau would continue to be funded by other organizations.

IDAC received a small grant to cover the expenses of an exploratory trip to Guinea-Bissau. When we returned, I talked a great deal about the work we conducted there. The introduction to *Letters to Guinea-Bissau* is a methodological narration of our work during this trip. As you can see, the objectives of the literacy program were developed in Guinea-Bissau, not in Geneva, and they were developed largely by Guineans. Once this program had been developed, we obtained more financial assistance so we could continue to avoid burdening the government of Guinea-Bissau. (Incidentally, I was given the same sort of financial assistance when I went to Nicaragua. The Nicaraguan government did not pay for my trip. The same kind of arrangements were made for my trips to Angola and to São Tomé and Príncipe.)

Macedo: You mentioned that the literacy project in which you, along with other members of IDAC, contributed by providing technical assistance was fully developed in Guinea-Bissau and not in Geneva. However, you have been criticized for trying to implement a plan that was idealistic and populist, that ignored important political, economic, cultural, and linguistic factors that shaped the reality of Guinea-Bissau. Did you and your team from IDAC fully discuss and evaluate the reality of the Guinea-Bissau society before executing your plan?

Freire: I find this criticism scientifically inconsistent. In what way could the IDAC team and I have developed a populist literacy project in Guinea-Bissau? What is the meaning of a political style that is called "populist?" Political analysts say that a populist style necessarily requires the emergence of the popular masses who begin to want, at the very least, to have a different position in the social and political history of their society. It is as if the oppressed suddenly begin to discover the possibility of deviating from the complacent state in which they find themselves; they begin to see the possibility of taking different risks. Symbolically, one could say that before, in their immersion, the risks were preponderantly stagnant. Before, there were risks that only involved survival in the face of exploitation. In certain ways, the subordinate role of the oppressed was perceived as a result of climatic difficulties (for example, there is no rain; therefore we don't have any work or anything to eat) and not as calculated exploitation by the dominant class. During the emergence of oppressed people, they begin to take risks — the risk to say the word; the social, historical, and political risks involved in protesting. There are no clear reasons for this that emerge; maybe it is because of changes in the productive forces of society, because of a situation exacerbated by local members of the dominant class.

These people emerge by taking new and different risks — the risk to be arrested on the street, to go to jail. But there is also the counterrisk: the possibility of being heard. This provokes a response by means of a political style often called populism. Thus, we can say that the populist style of politics is more of an answer than a cause. It is not the populist style that provokes the rising up of oppressed people. It is the rising up of the people that makes politicians change their tactics to remain in power.

What happens then? This new style is given a name: populism. When the oppressed rise and the dominant classes need to defend themselves (to respond defensively to the rising up of the people while maintaining their power), the leadership that was called populist assumes an ambiguity that is manifested in the relationship between the emerging masses and the dominant classes. On the one hand, to continue to be populist, the leadership needs the support of the people on the street. On the other hand, it needs to establish limits in relation to the action of these people so that there is no rupture in the bourgeois style of politics and society in general. These limits are designed to prevent the transformation of society, so that the oppressed do not turn into revolutionaries. Thus, the dominant classes create obstacles to prevent the subordinate classes from transcending their class and gaining class consciousness.

What is the nature of this ambiguity? By limiting the demanding presence of the people, whereby people take to the streets and protest in the parks, the populist leadership cannot stop the people from learning how to use the streets and the parks to voice their demands. The populist leadership can limit its response to the demands of the people. But if it prohibits the people from assembling on the streets, the leadership stops being populist and becomes an overtly repressive regime. To the extent that it only limits its response to certain demands of the people (for example, by allowing demonstrations in designated areas only), it allows the continuance of public demonstrations, which will lead inevitably to an even greater process of discovery whereby the oppressed learn how to make demands. The people end up thriving and assuming their own demands. Thus, the populism that manipulates contradicts itself by stimulating democracy.

There is a point at which political leadership maintains itself by oscillating between manipulation and democratic experience. There is also a point at which the leadership can lean more toward the people. One dimension of its ambiguity has this leadership taking one step to the left and one to the right, with one foot atop the oppressed masses, the other atop the bourgeoisie. When this leadership begins to step with both feet on the masses, there are two possibilities. First, the society can fall into a prerevolution, the so-called populist leadership denouncing populism and entering into its own revolutionary process. Second, the right wing steps in with a coup and installs a rigid, military regime.

From a scientific point of view, which populist characteristics can one find in our involvement in Guinea-Bissau? Which populist aspects are there in our proposals in Guinea-Bissau for the reform of education in general, and adult literacy in particular? We were in contact with a political leadership that had spent years fighting the Portuguese colonialists in the jungles, without traces of populism.

What is the populist dimension of the letters I wrote to the educators of Guinea-Bissau? In the third and fourth letters, for example, where I examine the very serious aspects of dealing with the meaning of a socialist, revolutionary education, or where I discuss the relationship between education and production and the problem of the autonomy of the working class, where is the populist character in these published documents? My impression is that some people probably read the works of a famous Brazilian educator who criticizes me by characterizing me as a populist. Should I be characterized as such for making a contribution to my country under a populist regime?

Today in Brazil, for example, we have begun a historical new phase in political life. Even though I belong to a political party that did not participate in the development of this new government, as a Brazilian I sincerely hope that these democratic moves continue and the system undergoes the necessary transformations to benefit the working class. But no one would claim that Brazil's government is a revolutionary regime. Many of the educators criticizing me as populist are now making their contributions to Brazil's government. It would be interesting to see in ten or twenty years if students working on their theses, for example, would consider these educators populists even though they are contributing to a government that is far from revolutionary.

One is not necessarily populist because one makes certain contributions to a regime that is regarded as populist. Yet what I find even stranger is the claim that the proposals that I made to Guinea-Bissau in conjunction with the team from IDAC were populist. It would be just as ridiculous to characterize as populist my discussion with educators in Angola. There are people who even claim that I did nothing more than transplant my Brazilian experience to Guinea-Bissau. This is absolutely false.

I have also been accused of being indifferent to various ethnic groups in Guinea-Bissau. This is also ridiculous. Why would I reject the idea of learning more? By analyzing and studying the cultural and linguistic diversity in Guinea-Bissau, I was in a better position to comprehend the educational needs of Guinea-Bissau. What I could not do in Guinea-Bissau is overstep the political limitations of the moment. As a foreigner, I could not impose my proposals on the reality of Guinea-Bissau and on the needs as perceived by political leaders. For example, the linguistic question was one of the boundaries that I could not step over, although I fully and emphatically discussed with the educators my concerns about carrying out the literacy campaign in the language of the colonialists. However, the leadership found it politically advantageous to adopt the Portuguese language as the main vehicle in the literacy campaign.

Macedo: As an admirer of Amilcar Cabral, you could not ignore his detailed analysis of the cultural and linguistic character of Guinea-Bissau. Cabral himself showed great concern with respect to the probable difficulties during the postindependence period with the national unification process, given so many diverse ethnic groups.

Freire: Exactly. Amilcar Cabral was a thinker who put his thinking into practice. He was a thinker whom I read over and again and always get new perspectives from.

One of my dreams, which went unfulfilled, was to conduct a thorough analysis of Amilcar Cabral's work. I even have a title for the book that I wanted to write: Amilcar Cabral: The Pedagogue of the Revolution. In this book I would have drawn a clear distinction between "revolutionary pedagogue" and "pedagogue of the revolution." We have some revolutionary pedagogues; but we don't have many pedagogues of the revolution. Amilcar is one of them.

To accomplish this dream, however, I would have had to stay in Guinea-Bissau for at least six to eight months and also go to other African countries. I had neither the finances nor the time to carry out such an ambitious task. I would not ask the government of Guinea-Bissau to pay for my project, in view of the tremendous financial difficulties this new country faced in the reconstruction of its society after independence. I was also reluctant to ask the World Council of Churches to finance my project.

I did some preliminary work, such as conducting interviews with important political leaders who worked closely with Cabral. I interviewed the PAIGC leadership in Guinea-Bissau, for example. I said in one interview with the political director of the time that the project could not be carried out by an intellectual who considers himself objective and free to say whatever he or she wants. My idea was not to go into Guinea-Bissau to carry out research and later write a book in which I say what I might want to say under the rubric of so-called "academic autonomy" or "scientific objectivity." I am a militant intellectual. As such, I wanted to do a serious and rigorous study about Cabral as a pedagogue of the revolution.

But first I would have had to get to know how the party, which was founded by Cabral, and which fought courageously to expel the colonizers, viewed my plan. There were conditions I wanted to establish. If the project had gone forward, before I published the work I would have submitted the manuscript for review by the party. I would not have published the book without the party's approval.

Perhaps the leadership could have responded to my conditions by asking me why I was such an obedient intellectual. I would have said that I am not an "obedient" intellectual. For example, if PAIGC had told me that some of the things I stated were not in the interest of political reform, I would probably have fought with the party to defend my position. But I would also have appreciated the reasons that led the party to conclude that my statements were undermining their goals.

Only after this process would I have submitted the final draft for publication. All the royalties would have gone to political causes that would further advance the humanitarian and social justice that led to both the creation of the party in the first place and the subsequent revolution.

Unfortunately, I was not able to complete this study. I conducted approximately ten interviews, the first one with the minister of education, Mario Cabral. I also interviewed militant youth groups organized during the struggle for liberation. But because of time difficulties and other factors, I decided not to continue with the project. I was thinking of conducting about 300 interviews. Just the work involved in these interviews, the transcriptions of the tapes, the selection and editing of the transcriptions, would have taken years to complete. I could have done the transcription and editing in Europe, but the interviews would have had to be done in Africa, mainly in Guinea-Bissau.

Talking to you about this stalled project highlights how I behaved with respect to the principles of the revolution. I respected the cultural and political autonomy of the people of Guinea-Bissau. I accept it as a fact when people say that I am incompetent in many areas. However, I never tried to succeed by means of criticizing other people's incompetence. That is, by criticizing some people, this criticism could give me visibility and intellectual prestige.

In fact, I do not care about prestige. My major preoccupation is to work honestly and seriously toward the development of a better and just society, as I have done in Guinea-Bissau. If people read *Letters to Guinea-Bissau* they will see my commitment to the educational transformation in that country.

In the book that "talked" with my Chilean friend I made the following observation. In Brazil during the 1950s I defended the position that learners, no matter what level, should allow themselves to experiment with becoming subjects of the act of knowing, which education implies. Now I ask, how could I have done the contrary in Guinea-Bissau? Moreover, in the revolutionary context I must insist that learners become subjects, subjects of the reinvention of their country.

Where is this poor Brazilian educator's populism, an educator who insisted during his meetings with Guinean educators that the people should march and assume their country's history? Have you ever heard a populist talk about the rights of learners to become subjects and assume their history? Ask Fernando Cardenal and Ernesto Cardenal if my work and suggestions for Nicaragua were of a populist nature. These criticisms reveal how superficially my critics have approached my writing. Their brand of ideology prevents them from understanding or wanting to understand the pedagogical proposals I have advanced.

Macedo: How would you confront the process of emancipation through literacy in a society characterized by difficulties rooted in the presence of multiple discourses? This problem becomes infinitely more complex when the society is characterized by many competing languages, such as in Guinea-Bissau.

Freire: We first have to deal with the relationship between literacy and emancipation. The concept of literacy here should be taken as transcending its etymological content. Literacy cannot be reduced to experiences that are only a little creative, that treat the foundations of letters and words as a purely mechanical domain.

In answering your question I will try to go beyond this rigid comprehension of literacy and begin to understand literacy as the relationship of learners to the world, mediated by the transforming practice of this world taking place in the very general social milieu in which learners travel, and also mediated by the oral discourse concerning this transforming practice. This understanding of literacy takes me to a notion of a comprehensive literacy that is necessarily political.

Even in this global sense, literacy by itself should never be understood as the triggering of social emancipation of the subordinated classes. Literacy leads to and participates in a series of triggering mechanisms that need to be activated for the indispensable transformation of a society whose unjust reality destroys the majority of people. Literacy in this global sense takes place in societies where oppressed classes assume their own history. The most recent case of this type of literacy is in Nicaragua.

Interestingly, the nature of this process is different from that of emancipation. Literacy in the case of Nicaragua started to take place as soon as the people took their history into their own hands. Taking history into your own hands precedes taking up the alphabet. Anyone who takes history into his or her own hands can easily take up the alphabet. The process of literacy is much easier than the process of taking history into your own hands, since this entails the "rewriting" of your society. In Nicaragua the people rewrote their society before reading the word.

Further, it is interesting to observe that in cultural history the human being, or, more accurately, the animal that becomes human and the human being who is the result of this previous transformation, first changes the world and much later becomes capable of talking about the world that he or she has transformed. A much longer time elapses before he or she is able to write about the talk generated from this transformation. Literacy must be seen and understood in this global sense. Since the reading of the word is preceded by the rewriting of society in societies that undergo a revolutionary process, it is much easier to conduct successful literacy campaigns in these societies.

But all of this discussion is far more general, more political, and more historical than the literacy process itself. One cannot forget the specific dimension of the linguistic code. In the case of Nicaragua, the only problematic area of the linguistic code (which has its own necessarily ideological, social, and political implications) is the situation of the Mosquito Indians. For the rest, the big problem concerning the Spanish language is the multiple discourses you talked about. These discourses, in my view, are linked to the differences among the various social classes and can be appreciated only in light of class analyses.

The great problem that literacy campaigns face with respect to multiple discourses is dealing with the process of rewriting society. In principle, this rewriting breaks down the rigid hierarchical order of social classes and thereby transforms the material structures of society. Let me reemphasize one point: we should never take literacy as the triggering of social transformation. Literacy as a global concept is only a part of the transformative triggering mechanism. There is a difference of quality between a political crusade and the experience of literacy, even in Brazil today. I recall that in the world conference in Persepolis organized by UNESCO in 1975 — participating countries included the Soviet Union, the United States, Cuba, North Korea, Vietnam, Peru, Brazil, and numerous European countries — one of the central themes was the evaluation of literacy campaigns throughout the world. "The Letter of Persepolis," published by UNESCO, states, among other things, that the relative success of literacy campaigns evaluated by UNESCO depended on their relation to the revolutionary transformations of the societies in which the literacy campaigns took place.

This demonstrates the extraordinary role that the reading of the world and reality play in the general reinvention of education and the revolutionary society. It also shows that even in societies with great limitations due to their reactionary stance, for instance, although one would expect less successful results, a literacy campaign can still succeed and help other key factors trigger the transformation of this society. However, it is impossible and inadvisable to forget the linguistic issue.

Now, let's talk about the great problems that we had to confront in Guinea-Bissau.

Macedo: You can begin, I think, by addressing the linguistic challenges you encountered in Guinea-Bissau.

Freire: Guinea-Bissau met the first basic condition that makes the success of literacy campaigns possible: the revolutionary transformation of society. Guinea-Bissau had completed a long and beautiful struggle for liberation, under the uncontested leadership of the extraordinary pedagogue Amilcar Cabral. (In *Letters to Guinea-Bissau* I often refer to the pedagogical aspect of Cabral's leadership, the seminars he conducted during the struggle, not only to evaluate military successes, but also the cultural struggle.)

In brief, Guinea-Bissau had the political, social, and historical contexts, namely the struggle on the part of its people to liberate themselves. But Guinea-Bissau did not meet the second condition, due to its linguistic diversity. Guinea-Bissau has about thirty different languages and dialects spoken by various ethnic groups. In addition, it has Creole, which functions as a lingua franca. Creole gives Guinea-Bissau, Cape Verde, and São Tomé an enormous advantage over Angola and Mozambique, for example.

Creole, a linguistic creation that combines African languages and Portuguese, developed gradually in Guinea-Bissau. Creole is to Portuguese what Portuguese, Spanish, French, and Italian are to Latin: a descendent. Creole is as beautiful and rich and viable as Portuguese. No linguistic expression or language is born ready-made. For example, there is no need for Portuguese, Germans, and Spaniards to be ashamed of using a word like *estress* (stress), which is directly borrowed from English. I do not know any other possible word for stress in Portuguese. The development of the productive forces of technology and science have a great deal to do with linguistic development as well. We have to accept [or *stress*] hundreds of such words, *know-how* for instance.

We see Brazilian products made in Brazil that say, in English, "Made in Brazil." This commonplace wording internationalizes communication. I am not ashamed of using such terms. Thus, should Creole speakers be ashamed if they borrow certain terms from the Portuguese language to address the technological development of their society?

You cannot establish by decree the inviability of such development. And this is, more or less, what I said to the commission on education. At the peril of being misinterpreted by the president's security guard, I put my hands on Luis Cabral's head and said, "Mr. President, I understand why you get headaches when you speak Portuguese for a long time. The fact is, your mental structure is not Portuguese, even though you speak Portuguese very well. Your thinking structure, which deals with the way you talk and express yourself, is not Portuguese."

There was a Guinean newspaper, *No Pintcha*, that at that time customarily printed one of Amilcar Cabral's texts in every issue. *No Pintcha* played an important role in disseminating Cabral's ideas. By an odd coincidence, the day following my speech *No Pintcha* printed the only Amilcar Cabral speech with which I disagree. In it he said that the most beautiful gift the Portuguese left Guineans was the Portuguese language. (Cabral's statement should be interpreted in the context of the struggle for liberation. In fact, I learned later that there were political reasons for Cabral's statement. Cabral was trying to use Portuguese as a unifying force to calm the friction between the competing linguistic and ethnic groups in Guinea-Bissau.) I read Cabral's text as a direct message to me: "My comrade Paulo Freire, we like you very much, but don't butt into this business of language in our country. Amilcar Cabral himself said that Portuguese was a beautiful gift from the colonizers."

Notwithstanding this message, I continued to fight, along

with the members of IDAC, about the role of Portuguese in the literacy campaign. An IDAC colleague, Marcos Arruda, fought intensely over the language issue. We finally were able to bring to Guinea-Bissau two linguists (one Belgian, the other African, also financed by IDAC) to discuss and evaluate the linguistic dilemma in Guinea-Bissau. Both were from the Language Institute of Dakar. The Belgian was a specialist in Creole languages; the African a specialist in African languages. At the same time I contacted a Brazilian linguist who taught in Leon and was a specialist in Creole languages. (He was working on a dictionary and grammar of Creole in Guinea-Bissau.) He never came to Guinea-Bissau, but we discussed at great length the issues of language in Guinea-Bissau.

We proposed to Mario Cabral a seminar in Guinea-Bissau that would include the five African countries liberated from Portuguese colonialism. The purpose of this seminar would be to discuss the politics of language planning and literacy training in their respective countries. We wanted to see a general discussion about the politics of culture, within which you find the politics of language.

It was at this seminar that I became absolutely convinced that Portuguese could never be a viable language in the literacy campaign. I then wrote a letter to Mario Cabral (see Appendix) in which I reiterated the impossibility of continuing to do literacy work in Portuguese. In this letter I also analyzed the consequences of insisting upon using Portuguese as the only vehicle of education. One consequence, for instance, is that while Portuguese would function as the official language, it would have to assume the role of the national languages as well.

Why? To the extent that you expect a language given official status to become the mediating force in the education of youth, you are understandably asking this language to assume the role of national language. It would be inconceivable to expect Brazil, for example, to adopt Spanish as the only language of education if Brazil were to undergo a revolutionary process, Cuban-style, or in another example that might better serve the interest of the Brazilian bourgeoisie, to implement English as the sole language of instruction and business.

In my letter to Mario Cabral I said that the exclusive use of

Portuguese in education would result in a strange experience characterized by Portuguese as a superstructure that would trigger an exacerbation of class divisions, and this in a society that was supposed to be re-creating itself by breaking down social classes.

To continue to use Portuguese in Guinea-Bissau as the mediating force in the education of youth and to continue the practice of selecting students on the basis of their knowledge of spoken and written Portuguese would guarantee that only the children of the elite would be able to advance educationally, thus reproducing an elite, dominant class. The people of Guinea-Bissau would again find themselves locked out of the educational system and higher economic and political echelons. For these reasons I made proposals for an alternative to using Portuguese as the language of instruction.

Macedo: Why didn't you include in *Letters to Guinea-Bissau* the letter you wrote to Mario Cabral in 1977, in which you raised these concerns about the role of Portuguese in the literacy campaign?

Freire: I did not include this letter for political reasons, among other things. I knew that in Guinea-Bissau, as well as in Cape Verde, the question of the Portuguese language in education was not only a problem, but also was not discussed openly. I was familiar with the high level of ideology regarding the issue of language. This was easy to understand, given that the Portuguese colonizers spent centuries convincing the people of Guinea-Bissau that their languages were ugly and that Portuguese was more cultivated.

The colonizers spent centuries trying to impose their language. They did this by decree, giving the impression that the national languages were naturally inferior, that they were only tribal dialects. Creole was also viewed as a mixed and corrupted jargon, and thus could not be considered a natural language. This profile was established by colonizers (only those in power can profile others) and forced upon the people of Guinea-Bissau; and it was never rejected, even during the war for liberation. Many leaders of Guinea-Bissau were still influenced by these myths while being linguistically assimilated and colonized.

One of my great struggles in these ex-Portuguese colonies was to affirm the viability of the national languages. I am reminded of a radio debate I had in São Tomé in which the minister of education stated that the language of education in São Tomé had to be the Portuguese of Camões.* I remember responding to him by saying that even in Lisbon today one cannot teach the Portuguese of Camões, much less in São Tomé, where the majority of people do not even speak or understand Portuguese.

To a certain extent, I respected the divisions among these ex-colonies regarding language planning because I am not an imperialist. But I never missed an opportunity to let them know my real concerns about the role of Portuguese in education.

I did not publish the letter I had written to Mario Cabral because, as I have said, I felt the timing was not appropriate with respect to greater political concerns. I remember that in the last conversation I had with President Luis Cabral before he was ousted, he said: "Comrade Paulo, I can understand the controversy among ourselves concerning the language issue." I said that I understand the negative reactions of many of the leaders regarding national languages, but that it is necessary to have courage. It is necessary, in fact, to tell the world that you are not going to do to your own people what even the Portuguese colonizers could not do. That is, you should not attempt to eradicate the national languages and impose Portuguese. You need to take a stand and abandon the notion of teaching the Portuguese alphabet, so to speak.

I could not have said these things in public at that time. Today I can say them.

Macedo: Are you sorry for not having taken a public position on the linguistic issue in Guinea-Bissau?

Freire: No, because often there are reasons of a political character that require silence from the intellectual, even if this silence is sometimes misinterpreted. I assumed this silence and today I have broken it because I believe now is the time to talk about these issues. With or without Paulo Freire it was impossible in Guinea-Bissau to conduct a literary campaign in a language that

*An illustratious Portuguese poet (1524–1580) and the author of the Portuguese masterpiece *Os Lusíadas*.

was not part of the social practice of the people. My method did not fail, as has been claimed. Nor did it fail in Cape Verde or São Tomé. In São Tomé and Cape Verde there is a history of bilingualism. And even though bilingualism was less prevalent in Cape Verde than in São Tomé, it was still possible to learn some Portuguese with or without my help.

This issue should be analyzed in terms of whether it is linguistically viable to conduct literacy campaigns in Portuguese in any of these countries. My method is secondary to this analysis. If it is not viable to do so, my method or any other method will certainly fail. The letter to Mario Cabral (included in the Appendix) analyzes the viability of the Portuguese language, as well as the political and cultural consequences if a linguistic colonialization were to continue in this newly liberated nation.

Macedo: One problem some evaluators have in considering your work is that they ask technocratic questions, ignoring the political, cultural, and ideological dimensions of both your theories and practices. It could be that they overemphasize the mechanical acquisition of reading while they fail to assess the development of a critical attitude on the part of learners, that is, the extent to which learners in literacy campaigns become aware of their civic and political responsibilities. For example, to what extent do learners acquire an analytical attitude toward authority in their own daily existence? One should not apply quantitative means and methods to measure results that by their nature are qualitative. Can you comment more specifically on this evaluation problem?

Freire: First, in any evaluation of our involvement and contribution, the question to be asked should not be whether twenty, thirty, a hundred, a thousand, or more people mechanically learned how to spell in the Portuguese language. On the contrary, such an evaluation has to consider the extent to which we are also learned in the process of our involvement. For instance, one learns how difficult it is to remake a society, whether through revolution or otherwise; one cannot remake, reinvent, or reconstruct a society by means of a mechanical act. The reinvention of a society is a political act taking place in history. It is thus important to inquire into the difficulties of the reinvention of the society of Guinea-Bissau. It is also important to ask whether our involvement had any significance for the political educators of Guinea-Bissau.

Again, in this book I wrote with Faundes where I address some of these questions and criticisms about my work in Guinea-Bissau, I said that one day I would like to return to Guinea-Bissau and find the same openness, camaraderie, and political dimensions as before. I would like to return and talk with Mario Cabral, who received me with open arms. I would like to talk with all those comrades with whom I worked. I would ask them if, in our previous meetings and dialogues, some of our concerns had touched them. I would also ask them if these concerns had any impact on the reformulation of the educational process in Guinea-Bissau, as I believe this to be an important part of my evaluation.

Speaking of evaluation, I would again insist that the so-called failure of our work in Guinea-Bissau was not due to the "Freire method." This failure clearly demonstrated the inviability of using Portuguese as the only vehicle of instruction in the literary campaigns. This is a fundamental point.

The importance of our involvement should be measured against examples such as the one I used in my letter to Mario Cabral. A Guinean team was conducting an evaluation of the production work on the collective farm that they had created. One of the participants said in his native language (which was translated into Portuguese for me): "Before we did not know that we knew. Now we know that we knew. Because we today know that we knew, we can know even more."

This is such a discovery, such an affirmation, that it immediately becomes political and requires a political posture on the part of this man in the more general process of the reinvention of his country. This affirmation has to do with a critical theory of knowledge, resulting from the inviability of spelling in the Portuguese language. Among other things, this man discovered that he did not know before that he knew, but that now, for this reason, he discovered that he can know much more. I have asked myself what could have more value in a general evaluation of society that begins to find itself struggling against the colonizers.

A rapid and mechanical codification of the Portuguese language certainly could not have the same weight as the political awareness that was achieved during our debates on the learning of Portuguese. The mastery of the Portuguese alphabet does not compare with the political, epistemological comprehension of this man's presence in the world as a human being who can now know why he transforms himself. Without negating the probable need to master Portuguese or, even better, his own language, I cannot underestimate the significance of the second order of knowledge that this man acquired.

This is true precisely because there is no pedagogical experience that is not political in nature. This man's statements have great importance whether they are evaluated from a pedagogical or political perspective. To forget or, more manipulatively, to omit this critical aspect from the evaluation surpasses the limits of "ba-be-bi-bo-bu"; pure decodification of syllables are meaningless to those who have played a huge role in the reinvention of their society. The challenging task of reappropriating their culture and history could not be achieved through the language that negated their reality and attempted to eradicate their own means of communication.

Macedo: Do you think it is possible to conduct a literacy campaign in Portuguese in Cape Verde, where there is some degree of bilingualism in Portuguese and Creole?

Freire: From the political point of view it is not advisable to do so, for the many reasons we have already discussed. From the linguistic point of view, unlike Guinea-Bissau, where teaching in Portuguese is not possible, in Cape Verde it would be less violent to do so, particularly in urban areas, where the colonialist presence brought about some exposure to the Portuguese language and capitalist development required people to learn some Portuguese. I think, however, that Cape Verde should also opt for Creole as the official national language.

Macedo: We should not lose sight of the danger of reproducing those colonialist values that were, and still are, inculcated through the use of Portuguese. I believe it is impossible to re-Africanize the people through the medium that de-Africanized them. Even if it made sense linguistically (and I feel strongly that it does not), in political terms, any decision to continue to use Portuguese as the official language and the only vehicle of instruction in Cape Verde would seriously undermine the political goals set forth by Amilcar Cabral.

Freire: Then the ideal situation would be to stop literacy in Portuguese, attempt to accelerate the development of Creole, particularly the standardization of its written form, and begin gradually to substitute Creole for Portuguese as the language of instruction. Obviously this could not be done all at once. Just imagine the capital required to change the entire educational system overnight. Cape Verde would have to quickly translate into Creole all of the basic texts required by the curriculum. All of the texts on geography, reading, math, and science would have to be translated. Even teacher training in Creole would be no small accomplishment. But as in Tanzania, one could begin slowly to replace Portuguese through a transitional bilingual model in which Creole would play a greater role in education, while Portuguese would diminish considerably over time. Creole could be used effectively, for example, in the first ten years of schooling.

In this way, at some point you could substitute Creole for Portuguese in the early years of schooling and gradually Creole would be introduced in increasing amounts in all areas of the curriculum. This is what Tanzania did when they replaced English with Swahili. I am not sure whether Swahili is used today at the university level in Tanzania, but my impression is that primary and secondary education is conducted mostly in Swahili.

In any case, I think instruction in Creole is required, even from the perspective of those productive forces that may need Portuguese. And, of course, the people of Guinea-Bissau and Cape Verde can continue to learn Portuguese as a foreign language. But to take it for granted that Portuguese is the national language and the only vehicle for education is totally absurd. In São Tomé, where the degree of bilingualism is much higher than in Cape Verde, it would be somewhat easier. Even in the rural areas of São Tomé people seem to converse more easily in

Portuguese. This could be attributed to the small size of the island.

Macedo: The issue of language instruction hides myriad problems that have led to the creation of a neocolonialist literacy campaign in Cape Verde and Guinea-Bissau under the guise of eliminating illiteracy. Even if literacy training in Portuguese were totally viable, we need to raise the crucial question as to what extent, whether successful or not, the continued use of Portuguese would debase the literacy campaign as well as the cultural capital of subordinate Cape Verdians. The debate over the viability of Portuguese as a vehicle for literacy in Cape Verde rests on the technical issue of whether Cape Verdian Creole is a valid and rule-governed system. I think the question to be raised has to be infinitely more political. We need to question the resistance to literacy in Creole supported by claims that Creole lacks a uniform orthography. Excuses like this are used to justify the present policy of using Portuguese as the only medium of instruction. We should ask why Cape Verdian Portuguese speakers rely on the common argument that Portuguese has international status and therefore guarantees upward mobility for Portuguese-speaking educated Cape Verdians. This position, by the way, implies the supposed superiority of the Portuguese language.

The sad reality is that while Portuguese may offer access to certain positions of political and economic power for high echelons of Cape Verdian society, it holds back the majority of the people, those who fail to learn Portuguese well enough to acquire the necessary level of literacy for social, political, and economic advancement. In fact, to continue to use the language of the colonizer as the only medium of instruction is to continue to provide manipulative strategies that support the maintenance of cultural domination. Thus, what is hidden in the technical debate concerning Cape Verdian language instruction is a resistance to re-Africanization, or perhaps a subtle refusal on the part of assimilated Cape Verdians to "commit class suicide." If we are to understand fully the political and ideological factors underlying the language issue, we must reorient our questions from a technical level to a more political level. Can you evaluate the political and ideological consequences of teaching only in Portuguese in Cape Verde?

Freire: This is a political question rooted in ideology. When I was in Cape Verde, President Aristides Pereira gave an excellent speech in which he said, "We threw the Portuguese colonialists out of our land and now we need to decolonialize our mentality." The decolonialization of mentality is much more difficult to achieve than the physical expulsion of colonialist. Sometimes the colonizers are thrown out but they remain culturally, because they have been assimilated into the minds of the people they leave behind.

This terrible presence haunts the revolutionary process, and, in some cases, it hinders the movement toward liberation. Language does not remain unaffected. The more this colonialist presence haunts the assimilated spirits of the colonized people, the more they will reject their own language. In fact, language is so much a part of culture that by rejecting it, the reappropriation of one's culture becomes a revolutionary illusion.

The ex-colonialized in many ways continue to be mentally and culturally colonized. The colonized people were told either verbally or through message systems inherent in the colonial structure that they did not possess effective cultural instruments with which to express themselves. They possessed an ugly dialect, a bastardization of the colonial language. This language profile imposed by the colonizers eventually convinced the people that their language was in fact a corrupt and inferior system unworthy of true educational status.

People end up believing that the way they speak is savage. They become ashamed of speaking their own language, particularly in the presence of the colonialists who constantly proclaim the beauty and superiority of their own language. The colonizers' behaviors and tastes, including language, are the models that were imposed by the colonial structure over centuries of oppression. At some point the ex-colonialized internalize these myths and feel ashamed.

I remember a story you told me concerning a Cape Verdian who vehemently denied that he spoke Creole, but at parties constantly sang in Creole. When confronted with the fact that if he sang Creole so well he must also speak it, he defensively stated that he only knew how to sing but not speak Creole. Maybe he was not aware of it, but he was totally assimilated into the cultural value system of the colonialists. He was convinced that he did not speak his own native language. In fact, he forbade himself to speak his own language. This process is sometimes unconscious. It is the colonializers' ghost whispering in his ears, "Your language is no good . . . it is savage."

You are absolutely right in your analysis of the language issues in ex-colonialized countries. I have always said in my conversations with the people of Guinea-Bissau, Cape Verde, São Tomé, Angola, and Mozambique that the expression "Portuguese Africa" is a misnomer. When intellectuals from these countries use the term, I always tell them that there is no Africa of the Portuguese, nor of the French, nor of the English. There is an Africa upon which the Portuguese language was imposed at the expense of the native languages. If viewed from this perspective, the notion of Portuguese Africa hides the true linguistic issue.

I think we can safely say that in exceptional cases Cape Verdians should study Portuguese, but only as a second language.

6

The Illiteracy of Literacy in the United States

Macedo: It is ironic that in the United States, a country that prides itself on being the first and most advanced within the so-called "first world," over 60 million people are illiterate or functionally illiterate. According to Jonathon Kozol's book *Illiterate America* (1985), the United States is in forty-ninth place among the 128 countries of the United Nations in terms of literacy rate. How can a country that considers itself a model of democracy tolerate an educational system that contributes to such a high level of illiteracy?

Freire: The first reaction to these data should be one of shock. How can this be possible? But this would still be a reaction at the affective level. Let us think a bit about this phenomenon. The first question might be, did this huge sector of the population, the illiterate or functionally illiterate, ever go to school? In Latin America you have a number of people who are illiterate because they were socially forbidden to go to school. And you have another large population of illiterates who went to school. If this large illiterate sector of the population never went to school, the shock that I mentioned before is exacerbated by the immense contradiction this implies, given the United States' high level of modernization. Further, we have to consider whether illiterates did go to school and whether they were untouched by the school to the extent that they remained illiterate (apparently they were not touched, but, actually, they *were* touched), and whether they left school or they were left by the school.

I am inclined to think that this large population of illiterates in the United States went to school and then were expelled from school. How were they expelled? Were they thrown out by decree because they did not learn how to read and write? I believe that the school did not operate in this overt a manner.

This brings us to a point that is once again political and ideological in nature. And let us not forget the question of power, which is always associated with education. Our speculations should provoke those who are in the school systems to react to the following notion as absurd, nonrigorous, and purely ideological. The notion is: this large number of people who do not read or write and who were expelled from school do not represent a failure of the schooling class; their expulsion reveals the triumph of the schooling class. In fact, this misreading of responsibility reflects the schools' hidden curriculum. (Henry Giroux has written brilliantly on this subject, and I urge readers to consult his work.)

Curriculum in the broadest sense involves not only the programmatic contents of the school system, but also the scheduling, discipline, and day-to-day tasks required from students in schools. In this curriculum, then, there is a quality that is hidden and that gradually incites rebelliousness on the part of children and adolescents. Their defiance corresponds to the aggressive elements in the curriculum that work against the students and their interests.

School authorities who repress these students might argue that they are only responding to the students' aggressiveness. In fact, students are reacting to a curriculum and other material conditions in schools that negate their histories, cultures, and day-to-day experiences. School values work counter to the interests of these students and tend to precipitate their expulsion from school. It is as if the system were put in place to ensure that these students pass through school and leave it as illiterates.

This type of thinking typifies many well-intentioned educators who are not yet able to comprehend the internal mechanisms of the dominant ideology that so influences the school atmosphere. Because of the rebelliousness of children and adolescents who leave school or who are truants and refuse to engage in the intellectual activity predetermined by the curriculum, these students end up refusing to comprehend the word (not their own word, of course, but the word of the curriculum). They thus remain distant from the practice of reading.

Macedo: Let's clarify what you refer to as intellectual activity from the dominant point of view, so as not to preclude other intellectual activities that are generated and sustained by these students. We should emphasize that these students can, and in fact do, engage in frequent intellectual activities, but these are activities generated from their own perspective. That is, they define their own activities.

Freire: It is difficult to understand these issues outside of an analysis of power relations. Only those who have power, for example, can define what is correct or incorrect. Only those who have power can decide what constitutes intellectualism. Once the intellectual parameters are set, those who want to be considered intellectuals must meet the requirements of the profile dictated by the elite class. To be intellectual one must do exactly what those with the power to define intellectualism do.

The intellectual activity of those without power is always characterized as nonintellectual. I think this issue should be underscored, not just as a dimension of pedagogy, but a dimension of politics, as well. This is difficult to do in a society like that of the United States, where the political nature of pedagogy is negated ideologically. It is necessary to negate the political nature of pedagogy to give the superficial appearance that education serves everyone, thus assuring that it continues to function in the interest of the dominant class.

This mythical universality of education to better serve humanity leads many to blame the students themselves for dropping out. It is their decision if they want to remain and succeed in school.

Once you accept the political dimension of education, it becomes difficult to accept the education, it becomes difficult to accept the dominant class's conclusion: that the dropouts are to blame. The more you deny the political dimension of education, the more you assume the moral potential to blame the victims. This is somewhat paradoxical. The many people who pass through school and come out illiterate because they resisted and refused to read the dominant word are representative of self-affirmation. This self-affirmation is, from another point of view, a process of literacy in the normal, global sense of the term. That is, the refusal to read the word chosen by the teacher is the realization on the part of the student that he or she is making a decision not to accept what is perceived as violating his or her world.

In the end, what you have is a separation between teacher and students along class lines. Even though we recognize that it is very difficult to do an analysis of class in a complex society like that of the United States, we cannot deny that class division exists.

Macedo: In general, educators in the United States deemphasize the issue of social class as it pertains to education. In fact, most of the studies concerning the unacceptable number of illiterates in the school system treat the problem from a technocratic perspective. And the remedies proposed tend to be technocratic as well. Although some educators may describe a possible correlation between the high dropout rate and the low socioeconomic background of students, this correlation remains at a level of description. More often than not, U.S. educators in general and literacy experts in particular fail to establish political and ideological linkages in their analyses that could illuminate the reproductive nature of schools in this society. For example, conservative educators such as Secretary of Education William Bennett call for a back-to-basics approach as they blindly embrace competency-based curricula. Although the rigidity of the competency-based approach may benefit the white- and upper-class students, I doubt that it will remedy the illiteracy problem that plagues the majority of subordinate groups in the United States. Panaceas such as more student-contact hours for reading and math and a better salary base for teachers will perpetuate those ideological elements that negate students' life experiences. As a result, students react by refusing to read what the curriculum has decided they should read.

There is no guarantee that more of the same approach, which fundamentally lacks equity and sensitivity for the culture of the subordinate groups, will diminish the resistance of students as they refuse to read the "chosen" word. When curriculum designers ignore important variables such as social-class differences, when they ignore the incorporation of the subordinate cultures' values in the curriculum, and when they refuse to accept and legitimize the students' language, their actions point to the inflexibility, insensitivity, and rigidity of a curriculum that was designed to benefit those who wrote it.

By giving teachers token salary increases, one is paternalistically placating the majority of teachers, who find themselves in an increasingly powerless position as they confront a reductionist system that aims to further de-skill them. These approaches and their related proposals tend to overlook the material conditions with which teachers struggle in their attempt to survive the overwhelming task of teaching material that is politically and ideologically at odds with the subordinate students' reality.

These approaches and proposals fail to examine the lack of time teachers have to perform a task that, by its very nature, should involve thinking and reflection. Moreover, the intellectual dimension of teaching is never celebrated by a system whose main objective is to further de-skill teachers and reduce them to mere technical agents who are destined to walk unreflectively through a labyrinth of procedures. So my question is, do you think that these educators are aware that their proposals will exacerbate the equity gap that is already victimizing a great number of "minority" students?

Freire: Let's first clarify the term "minority."

Macedo: I use the term in the U.S. context. I am also aware that it is contradictory in nature.

Freire: Exactly. Do you see how ideologically impregnated the term "minority" is? When you use "minority" in the U.S. context to refer to the majority of people who are not part of the dominant class, you alter its semantic value. When you refer to "minority" you are in fact talking about the "majority" who find themselves outside the sphere of political and economic dominance.

Macedo: If Kozol is correct, the 60 million illiterates and functional illiterates that he documents in *Illiterate America* do not constitute a minority class. These 60 million should not be added to other sizable groups who learn how to read but who are still not part of dominant political and economic spheres.

Freire: In reality, as with many other words, the semantic alteration of the term "minority" serves to hide the many myths that are part of the mechanism sustaining cultural dominance.

Macedo: Let us move on to our second question. I think it is of paramount importance to analyze how subordinate cultures are produced in the classroom. We need to understand the antagonistic relationships between subordinate cultures and the dominant values of the curriculum. Take, for example, the resistance to speaking the required standard dialect of the curriculum. The dominant curriculum is designed primarily to reproduce the inequality of social classes, while it mostly benefits the interests of an elite minority. How can North American progressive educators capitalize on the antagonistic cultural elements produced in subordinate students' acts of resistance, and how can educators launch a literacy campaign that would enable students to comprehend their world so they can later read it? That is, is it possible to use students' rebelliousness as a platform from which they can transcend the mechanistic nature of literacy imposed on them by a curriculum that demands only the mechanical codification and decodification of graphemes and phonemes to form words that further alienate them?

Freire: Your question is absolutely fundamental. Theoretically, the answer to it is of value not only in the U.S. context, but also in the Brazilian context, as well as in other areas where there are clear class divisions and tensions. The major difference lies in how to design and implement programs that meet the different needs of each context. I would find it easier to answer

your question within the Brazilian context. At any rate, theoretically your question necessarily takes us to the important issue
of whether it is possible to develop a critical literacy program
within the institutional space, which contradicts and neutralizes
the fundamental task required by the dominant power of the
schools. That is, we need to discuss the reproduction of the
dominant ideology, an important issue that has been clearly and
amply discussed by Henry Giroux and other North American
educators, as well.

Theories of reproduction tend to fall into a type of mechanical
exaggeration in which they interpret the real and concrete fact
that the educational system reproduces dominant ideology.
Within the educational system there is another task to be executed by conscious educators, independent of the wishes of the
dominant class. The educational task, from the perspective of
the dominant class, is to reproduce its ideology. But the educational task that contradicts the reproductionist process cannot
be carried out by anyone who opts for the status quo. This task
has to be carried out by the educator, who in fact refuses to
maintain the inequality inherent within the status quo.

The progressive educator rejects the dominant values imposed on the school because he or she has a different dream,
because he or she wants to transform the status quo. Naturally,
transforming the status quo is much more difficult to do than
maintaining it. The question that you raised has to do exactly
with this theory. As I have said, the educational space reproduces the dominant ideology. However, it is possible within
educational institutions to contradict imposed dominant values.

The reproduction of the dominant ideology necessarily implies an opaque reality. The unveiling of reality falls within the
space for possible change in which progressive and politically
clear educators must operate. I believe that this space for change,
however small, is always available. In the United States, where
society is much more complex than in Brazil, the task of em-
phasizing reality is more difficult. In this process it is necessary
for educators to assume a political posture that renounces the
myth of pedagogical neutrality.

These educators cannot reduce themselves to being pure education specialists. They cannot be educators who are concerned

with only the technical dimensions of bilingualism, for example, without a thorough understanding of the political and ideological implications of bilingualism and multiculturalism in the United States. Educators must become conscious individuals who live part of their dreams within their educational space.

Educators cannot work successfully by themselves; they have to work collaboratively in order to succeed in integrating the cultural elements produced by the subordinate students in their educational process. Finally, these educators have to invent and create methods in which they maximize the limited space for possible change that is available to them. They need to use their students' cultural universe as a point of departure, enabling students to recognize themselves as possessing a specific and important cultural identity.

The successful usage of the students' cultural universe requires respect and legitimation of students' discourses, that is, their own linguistic codes, which are different but never inferior. Educators also have to respect and understand students' dreams and expectations. In the case of black Americans, for example, educators must respect black English. It is possible to codify and decodify black English with the same ease as standard American English. The difference is that black Americans will find it infinitely easier to codify and decodify the dialect of their own authorship. The legitimation of black English as an educational tool does not, however, preclude the need to acquire proficiency in the linguistic code of the dominant group.

Macedo: Beyond the linguistic code issue, educators must understand the ways in which different dialects encode different world views. The semantic value of specific lexical items belonging to black English differs radically, in some cases, from the reading derived from the standard, dominant dialect. The first important issue is that black Americans' linguistic code not only reflects their reality, but also their lived experience in a given historical moment. Terms that encapsulate the drug culture, daily alienation, the struggle to survive the substandard and inhumane conditions of ghettos — these constitute a discourse black Americans find no difficulty in using.

It is from this raw and sometimes cruel reality that black

students can begin to unveil the obfuscation that characterizes their daily existence inside and outside the schools. Their language is, therefore, a powerful tool demystifying the distorted reality prepackaged for them by the dominant curriculum. As we will discuss in the last chapter of this book, language should never be understood as a mere tool of communication. Language is packed with ideology, and for this reason it has to be given prominence in any radical pedagogy that proposes to provide space for students' emancipation.

Freire: It is by the use of all dimensions of students' language, taste, and so forth that you and the students are able to arrive at the programmatic contents that attend to the immediate interests of those in power. You don't tell those in a dependent and oppressed position that, for example, they have no say in the substance of scientific study because this type of curricular requirement interests only students of the dominant class. Subordinate students also need the skills gained through studying the dominant curriculum. However, these skills should never be imposed at the sacrifice of a thorough understanding of reality, which enables students to develop a positive self-image before grappling with the type of knowledge that is outside their immediate world.

It is only after they have a firm grasp on their world that they can begin to acquire other knowledge. To acquire the selected knowledge contained in the dominant curriculum should be a goal attained by subordinate students in the process of self and group empowerment. They can use the dominant knowledge effectively in their struggle to change the material and historical conditions that have enslaved them. But they must never allow the knowledge that benefits the dominant class to domesticate themselves or, as in some cases, to turn them into little oppressors. The dominant curriculum must gradually become dominated by the dependent students so as to help them in their struggle for social equity and justice.

This vision is political and not merely *epistemological*. That is, in the case of black Americans, they need to master fully standard English in order to fight effectively for their preservation and their full participation in society. But that does not mean that standard American English is more beautiful or superior to black English. The notion of linguistic superiority is artificially imposed.

Macedo: Then standard English can be viewed as a weapon against the oppressive forces that use this dominant dialect as a way to maintain the present social order. We should also point out that critical mastery of the standard dialect can never be achieved fully without the development of one's voice, which is contained within the social dialect that shapes one's reality.

Freire: Exactly. This is what I mean by the necessary political and ideological dimensions in any pedagogy that proposes to be critical. The question of methods is directly linked to the creative and inventive capacity of political educators. Creativity obviously requires risk taking. The educational tasks that we have discussed so far can be carried out through a thorough understanding of the political and ideological nature of educators, and through a willingness to be creative and to take the risks that will allow this creativity to flourish. In highly modernized societies like that of the United States, I have noticed that people carry with them a long capitalistic historical experience that sustains a general theme of human existence always evolving from fear — the fear, for instance, of not getting tenure, the fear that conditions educators to be well behaved for many years so they can get tenure. Many years afterward, if they are not given tenure, they remain domesticated in fear of losing their second chance at tenure. If they are refused tenure, they become preoccupied only with trying to understand what possible misconduct led to the tenure denial. If they are granted tenure, of course, there is no reason to change the behavior for which they were bestowed the gift of tenure.

Macedo: I agree, but I think it is important to understand this fear of taking risks or being inventive, and the societal mechanisms that generate it. In some cases, mainstream educators sacrifice educational and moral principles to help sustain a status quo that they have identified as uncreative, just so they can receive the reward of tenure or personal social advancement. This compromise is connected to a lack of political clarity, which in the long run impedes any possibility for these educators to engage in an educational praxis leading to conscientization. Can you discuss this problem of political clarity among educators in highly modernized societies, such as the United States?

Freire: Before elaborating on what you refer to as "political clarity," let us first define this concept. I will try to explain what I sometimes refer to as "political clarity before an action," something necessary in the evolvement process of political praxis.

Our first concern has to do with the adverb *before* used in the expression "before an action." This *before* refers to a certain action, let us say action A, to be realized as a political task in the process of struggle and transformation. This *before* does not refer to just any form of action to achieve clarity in 'reading' reality. Its understanding requires us to prolong our critical and radical experience in the world. Understanding the world's sensibility does not take place outside our practice, that is, the lived practice or the practice upon which we reflect.

In the final analysis, what I have been calling "political clarity" cannot be found in the purely mechanical repetition, for example, of formal criticisms of U.S. imperialism or in the recitation (no less mechanical) of Marx's phrases. This type of intellectual posture does not relate to my notion of political clarity.

Political clarity is necessary for more profound engagement in political praxis, and it is emphasized in that praxis. This conception was well captured by Frei Betto, in a book we recently completed together in Brazil. According to Betto, a politicized person (a person who more or less has political clarity) is one who has transcended the perception of life as a pure biological process to arrive at a perception of life as a biographical, historical, and collective process.

In this moment, this person conceptualizes what Betto calls "a clothesline of information." On the clothesline we may have a flux of information and yet remain unable to link one piece of information with another. A politicized person is one who can sort out the different and often fragmented pieces contained in the flux. This person has to be able to sift through the flux of information and relate, for example, Pinochet and Reagan, or understand the ideological content of the term "freedom fighters" as it is applied to the *Contras* in their effort to sabotage the revolutionary process in Nicaragua. This person sees the ideology in the concept "terrorism" as applied to the military action against a cruel dictatorship that maintains a highly proficient death squad killing thousands of innocent women, children, and other civilians. Noam Chomsky, for instance, succinctly analyzes American policy in Latin America in *Turning the Tide*, pointing to the contradictions in the U.S. intervention.

Political clarity is possible to the extent that we reflect critically on day-to-day facts, and to the extent that we transcend our sensibilities (the capacity to feel them or to take notice of them) so as to progressively gain a more rigorous understanding of the facts. Even before this, still at the level of sensibility, we can begin to become clearer politically. This happens in Betto's biographical, historical, and collective process (described above).

For me, one of the possibilities we have working with a group of intellectuals, students, for example, is to challenge them to understand the social and historical reality, not of a given fact, but of a fact that is ongoing. Reality in this sense is the process of becoming.

We need to challenge students to understand that, as knowing subjects (sometimes of existing knowledge, sometimes of objects to be produced), our relation to knowable objects cannot be reduced to the objects themselves. We need to reach a level of comprehension of the complex whole of relations among objects. That is, we need to challenge them to treat critically the "clothesline of information" with which they are working.

Whether we work at the university level or in adult education literacy, whether involved in the pure sensibility of facts or in the pursuit of a more rigorous comprehension of facts, one of the difficulties in the critical treatment of the different "pieces" of information on the "clothesline" is that there are always obstacles that obfuscate political clarity. If it were not for these ideological obstacles, how could we explain the ease with which we accept President Reagan's pronouncements that a weak and poor country like Grenada poses a threat to the gigantic power of the United States?

Political clarity always implies a dynamic comprehension between the least coherent sensibility of the world and a more coherent understanding of the world. Through political practice the less coherent sensibility of the world begins to be surpassed and more rigorous intellectual pursuits give rise to a more coherent comprehension of the world. I find this transition to a more coherent sensitivity one of the fundamental moments in any educational praxis that attempts to go beyond the pure description of reality.

We need political clarity before we can understand the political action of eradicating illiteracy in the United States or any other place. Educators who do not have political clarity can, at best, help students read the word, but they are incapable of helping them read the world. A literacy campaign that enables students to read the world requires political clarity.

Macedo: Many educators in the United States have attempted to put into practice your theory of literacy. They often complain that you do not give any "how-to" information for putting into practice your theoretical ideas and your experiences in other areas of the world, particularly Africa and Latin America. First, do you find that these criticisms are valid? If not, can you address the anxieties of many well-intended educators who, perhaps, still feel captive to an educational culture of how-to manuals?

Freire: There are two parts to this question. The first refers to my reticence in telling educators what to do. The second deals with my lack of direction in the theories I have proposed.

Let's consider the first part. What is generated in any practice? Experiences and practices can be neither exported nor imported. It follows that it is impossible to fulfill someone's request to import practices from other contexts. How can a culture of a different history and historical time learn from another culture? How can a society learn from the experience of another, given that it is impossible to export or import practices and experiences?

When I ask these questions, I do not mean that it is impossible to learn from others' practices. Amilcar Cabral, who loved African culture, said that one's respect for African culture does not mean that one should ignore positive elements of other cultures, which may prove vital for the development of African culture. When I speak of the impossibility of exporting practices, I am not denying the validity of foreign practices. Nor am I negating the necessity for interchange. What I am saying is that they should be reinvented.

Macedo: Explain in concrete terms how one reinvents one's practice and experience.

Freire: You must have a critical approach to the practice and experience to be reinvented.

Macedo: What do you mean by a critical approach?

Freire: To approach others' practices and experiences critically is to understand the validity of social, political, historical, cultural, and economic factors relative to the practice and experience to be reinvented. In other words, reinvention demands the historical, cultural, political, social, and economic comprehension of the practice and proposals to be reinvented.

This critical process applies to the reading of books as well. For example, how can one apply Lenin to the Latin American context without making an effort to have a critical, political, and historical comprehension of the moment in which Lenin wrote? I cannot simply get by on Lenin's written text concerning a certain Russia at a certain time. In the preface to a new edition of his text, Lenin called attention to the necessity of having a critical comprehension of the moment in which he wrote the text. In our own case, it is also necessary to understand the historical, political, social, cultural, and economic moment, the concrete conditions that led Lenin to create the text in the first place. I cannot, then, simply use Lenin's text and apply it literally to the Brazilian context without rewriting it, without reinventing it.

Macedo: What would this rewriting consist of?

Freire: To the extent that I understand the parameters of the struggle in the Russia of Lenin's time, I can begin to understand what is happening in Brazil today. I can begin to see how valid certain general principles are so they can be reinvented. Other principles may have to be adapted for our context. I think it is impossible to read any text without a critical comprehension of the context to which the text refers.

Let's turn to your question of why I refuse to give so-called how-to recipes. When a North American educator reads my work, does not necessarily agree with all I say (he or she could not agree with me on everything, after all), but feels touched by my writings, rather than merely following me, he or she should begin practice by trying to critically comprehend the contextual conditions of where I worked. This educator must fully understand the economic, social, cultural, and historical conditions that culminated, for example, in the writing of *Pedagogy of the Oppressed*.

Educators must also investigate all of these conditions in their own contexts. When one thinks about the context that generated *Pedagogy of the Oppressed* and also thinks about one's own context, one can begin to re-create *Pedagogy of the Oppressed*. If educators are faithful to this radical reinvention, they will understand my insistence that learners assume the role of knowing subjects; that is, subjects who know alongside the educator, who is also a knowing subject. This is the principle of taking an epistemological, philosophical, pedagogical, and political stance.

It is one thing to read my work in order to identify with my positions and decide whether they are valid. But one ought not to do the same things I did in my practice.

In essence, educators must work hard so that learners assume the role of knowing subjects and can live this experience as subjects. Educators and learners do not have to do the exact same things I did in order to experience being a subject. That is because the cultural, historical, social, economic, and political differences that characterize two or more contexts will begin to play a role in the definition of the tense relationship between the educator and the learner, that is, the so-called values of a particular society. It is for this reason that I refuse to write a how-to manual or provide a step-by-step recipe.

I could not tell North American educators what to do, even if I wanted to. I do not know the contexts and material conditions in which North American educators must work. It is not that I do not know how to say what they should do. Rather, I do not know what to say precisely because my own viewpoints have been formed by my own contexts. I don't deny that I can make a contribution to U.S. educators. I think I have done so when visiting the United States and participating in concrete discussions with various groups about their projects. At these discussions I have suggested that, given my experience, I may be able to facilitate their work. But I cannot write a text that is filled with universal advice and suggestions.

When some educators criticize me on this point they reveal how influenced they are by the dominant ideology they are fighting against, and how they fail to understand the ways in which they reproduce it.

I once suggested to a group of U.S. students that they consider the following for their masters theses: how many texts were there in the United States in 1984, for instance, on how to make friends, get a good job, develop skills; that is, texts that primarily give recipes? These texts are explained in terms of the general context that generates them. There are many educators who welcome this type of text, which in essence contributes to further de-skilling. I refuse to write such texts, because my political convictions are opposed to the ideology that feeds such domestication of the mind.

For me, my major task in the United States, or elsewhere, is to say: Look, my political position is A, B, C. This political position requires that I maintain consistency between my discourse and my practice. This involves narrowing the distance between the two. Narrowing the distance between discourse and practice is what I call "coherence."

In any context I speak about my own practice, and upon reflection I articulate my practice theoretically. From here on, I have to challenge other educators, including those in my own country, to take my practice and my reflections as the object of their own reflections and analyze their context so they can begin to reinvent them in practice. This is my role as an educator; not to arrogantly pretend to be an educator of educators in the United States.

Macedo: This lack of coherence you talked about is a problem. Even though some North American educators agree with you theoretically, in practice they find themselves still conditioned by the dominant ideology. It could be that the failure to establish harmony between theory and practice leads to a head-on collision with the coherence necessary to maintain a succinct view of the political and pedagogical project at hand. It could be they unknowingly reproduce elements of the dominant ideology, which contradicts the fundamental principles of your theory.

Freire: Exactly. And this does not happen only in the United States, of course; it happens in Brazil as well. The distance that exists in Brazil between educators' revolutionary discourse and their practice is enormous. It is very common to find intellectuals who authoritatively discuss the right of the subordinated classes to liberate themselves. The mere act of talking about the working class as objects of their reflections smacks of elitism on the part of these intellectuals. There is only one way to overcome this elitism, which is also authoritarian and implies an inconsistency in intellectuals' revolutionary discourse. These intellectuals ought to stop speaking *about* and start speaking *with* the working classes. When educators expose themselves to the working classes, they automatically begin to become reeducated.

Macedo: They would also begin to understand and respect the cultural production of the working class; for example, their various forms of resistance as concrete aspects of culture.

Freire: Exactly.

Macedo: It is also important to stress, for instance, that the understanding of subordinated groups' cultural production is indispensable in any attempt to develop a type of emancipatory literacy. To do otherwise would be to develop pedagogical structures under the guise of a radical pedagogy that has hidden goals for assimilating students into ideological spheres of the dominant class. Critical to appreciating subordinated groups' culture is the element of resistance and how to use it as a platform that enables students to become literate in their own history and lived experiences.

Freire: You have touched upon an important point that Henry Giroux elaborates so eloquently in his writing: the problem of resistance. One of the learning tasks of educators who consider themselves progressive (for me, "revolutionary" is the preferred term) should be the critical comprehension of the different levels of resistance on the part of the subordinated classes, that is, the levels of their resistance given the levels of confrontation between them and the dominant classes.

Understanding these forms of resistance leads you to a better appreciation of their language; and, in fact, you cannot comprehend their resistance without grasping the essence of their language. Language makes explicit the ways in which people have been resisting. In other words, language gives you a glimpse of how people survive.

Understanding resistance leads to appreciating the "astuteness" of the oppressed classes as a way to defend themselves against the dominant. This astuteness is social to the degree that it is part of the social network of the oppressed class. This astuteness is explicit through the use of their language, artworks, music, and even in their physiology. The oppressed body develops immunization to defend itself against the harsh conditions to which it is subjugated. If this were not so, it would be impossible to explain how millions of Latin Americans and Africans continue to survive in subhuman conditions. Under similar conditions, you or I would not last more than a week. Our bodies have never had to develop the immune system to combat that type of harsh reality.

Again, understanding the oppressed's reality, as reflected in the various forms of cultural production — language, art, music — leads to a better comprehension of the cultural expression through which people articulate their rebelliousness against the dominant. These cultural expressions also represent the level of possible struggle against oppression.

For example, there are extraordinary murals and graffiti art in most U.S. cities populated by the working class and, more tragically, the jobless class. These are both cultural and political expressions. I visited Chicago with an artist who used these forms and he told me about black artists who paint on building walls depictions of the day-to-day existence of the oppressed classes. Though highly artistic and thus aesthetic, they are also a political act.

These artworks are an astute method that the dominated

classes use to denounce their unjust and often oppressive domination. They denounce through artistic expression and sometimes they hide their denunciation with artistic expression. It is this context of oppression that triggers the oppressed classes' need to be astute and to resist. Giroux is correct: any radical pedagogy must first understand fully the dynamics of resistance on the part of learners. Last year, for instance, an interesting book was published in Brazil: *The Feasts of the People: Pedagogy of Resistance*. The author analyzes various cultural expressions, people's different festive moments, not as pure folkloric expressions, but as cultural expressions through which they also express their resistance.

Cultural understanding from this point of view is fundamental for the radical educator. The basic difference between a reactionary and a radical educator relates to manifestations of resistance. The reactionary educator is interested in knowing the levels of resistance and the forms it takes so that he or she can smother this resistance. A radical educator has to know the forms and ways in which people resist, not to hide the reasons for resistance, but to explicate at the theoretical level the nature of this resistance.

Macedo: A radical educator should not remain at the level of theory exclusively. He or she should use resistance as a tool that will enable students to become literate in their culture as well as in the codes of the dominant classes.

Freire: The difference between reactionary and radical educators is that the reactionary wants to know about resistance to hide or suppress it, and the radical wants to know about resistance to understand better the discourse of resistance, to provide pedagogical structures that will enable students to emancipate themselves.

Macedo: Could you now address the second part of my question, on the lack of direction in your proposals.

Freire: As an educator, you can only maintain a nondirective posture if you attempt a deceitful discourse; that is, a discourse from the perspective of the dominant class. Only in this deceitful discourse can an educator talk about a lack of direction. Why?

I think this is because there is no real education without a directive. To the extent that all educational practice brings with it its own transcendence, it presupposes an objective to be reached. Therefore practice cannot be nondirective. There is no educational practice that does not point to an objective; this proves that the nature of educational practice has direction.

Let's now pose a question on epistemology and philosophy. The directional nature of educational practice that leads to a particular objective has to be lived by educators and learners. In other words, how can an educator behave in his educational practice in view of the directive nature of education? First, if this educator defends in practice the notorious position of those who wash their hands of such issues (somewhat like Pontius Pilate), he washes his hands and says in effect: "Since I respect students and I am not directive, and since they are individuals deserving respect, they should determine their own direction." This educator does not deny the directive nature of education that is independent of his own subjectivity. He simply denies himself the pedagogical, political, and epistemological task of assuming the role of a subject of that directive practice. He refuses to convince his learners of what he thinks is just. This educator, then, ends up helping the power structure.

What other viable methods are there relative to the directive nature of education? Another method would be to combat the situation I just described, that is, to combat laissez faire. The educator must help learners get involved in planning education, help them create the critical capacity to consider and participate in the direction and dreams of education.

The authoritarian educator is correct, even though he is not always theoretically explicit when he says that there is no education that is nondirective. I would not disagree with this educator; but I would say that he is authoritarian to the extent that he makes his own objectives and dreams the directives that he gives to learners in his educational practice. He is authoritarian because, as subject of the educational practice, he reduces learners to objects of the directives he imposes.

Which position or method is substantially democratic or, as I call it, radically democratic or revolutionary? The radically democratic view does not contain in its spontaneity the polar opposite of authoritarianism. After all, authoritarianism does not contain the polar opposite of spontaneity. For example, I am not going to be authoritarian so as not to be a laissez-faire educator. So as not to be an authoritarian, I am not going to be a laissez-faire educator.

Once more we fall into the theoretical framework of a pedagogical radicality as proposed by Giroux. We see that the correct way to assume the direction of education is to avoid reducing learners to a minority led by educators. On the contrary, the direction of education lies in the presentation of this problem to learners, a problem that is political, epistemological, and pedagogical. The problem of the directiveness and nature of education once more focuses on the issue of subjectivity, the role of education in the reconstruction of the world.

What are the roles of the educator and the learner? It cannot be merely that the learner follows the educator blindly. The role of an educator who is pedagogically and critically radical is to avoid being indifferent, a characteristic of laissez-faire educators. The radical has to be an active presence in educational practice. But the educator should never allow his or her active and curious presence to transform learners' presences into shadows of the educator's presence. Neither can the educator be the shadow of learners. The educator has to stimulate learners to live a critically conscious presence in the pedagogical and historical process.

Literacy and Critical Pedagogy

In the previous chapters we developed a view of literacy as a form of cultural politics. In our analysis, literacy becomes a meaningful construct to the degree that it is viewed as a set of practices that functions to either empower or disempower people. In the larger sense, literacy is analyzed according to whether it serves to reproduce existing social formations or serves as a set of cultural practices that promotes democratic and emancipatory change. We have not only provided a reconstructed theory of literacy, but also concrete, historical analyses of campaigns for literacy in countries such as Cape Verde, São Tomé and Príncipe, and Guinea-Bissau. In addition, we argued that the native languages of these countries must be used in literacy programs if literacy is to be an important part of an emancipatory pedagogy. In the cases we analyzed in detail, the use of Portuguese rather than the native African languages or Creole has led to the reproduction of a neocolonialist, elitist mentality. In this chapter, we will examine in more detail literacy programs in the light of theories of cultural production and reproduction. We will also argue more strongly for the use of the native language as a prerequisite to the development of any literacy campaign that purports to serve as the means to a critical appropriation of one's own culture and history.

141

Within the last decade, the issue of literacy has taken on a new importance among educators. Unfortunately, the debate that has emerged tends to recycle old assumptions and values regarding the meaning and usefulness of literacy. The notion that literacy is a matter of learning the standard language still informs the vast majority of literacy programs and manifests its logic in the renewed emphasis on technical reading and writing skills.

We want to reiterate in this chapter that literacy cannot be viewed as simply the development of skills aimed at acquiring the dominant standard language. This view sustains a notion of ideology that systematically negates rather than makes meaningful the cultural experiences of the subordinate linguistic groups who are, by and large, the objects of its policies. For the notion of literacy to become meaningful it has to be situated within a theory of cultural production and viewed as an integral part of the way in which people produce, transform, and reproduce meaning. Literacy must be seen as a medium that constitutes and affirms the historical and existential moments of lived experience that produce a subordinate or a lived culture. Hence, it is an eminently political phenomenon, and it must be analyzed within the context of a theory of power relations and an understanding of social and cultural reproduction and production. By "cultural reproduction" we refer to collective experiences that function in the interest of the dominant groups, rather than in the interest of the oppressed groups that are the object of its policies. We use "cultural production" to refer to specific groups of people producing, mediating, and confirming the mutual ideological elements that emerge from and reaffirm their daily lived experiences. In this case, such experiences are rooted in the interests of individual and collective self-determination.

This theoretical posture underlies our examination of how the public school systems in the ex-Portuguese colonies in Africa have developed educational policies aimed at stamping out the tremendously high illiteracy rate inherited from colonialist Portugal. These policies are designed to eradicate the colonial educational legacy, which had as its major tenet the total de-Africanization of these people. Education in these colonies was discriminatory, mediocre, and based on verbalism. It could not contribute anything to national reconstruction because it was not constituted for this purpose. Schooling was antidemocratic in its methods, in its content, and in its objectives. Divorced from the reality of the country, it was, for this very reason, a school for a minority and thus against the majority.

Before the independence of these countries in 1975, schools functioned as political sites in which class, gender, and racial inequities were both produced and reproduced. In essence, the colonial educational structure served to inculcate the African* natives with myths and beliefs that denied and belittled their lived experiences, their history, their culture, and their language. The schools were seen as purifying fountains where Africans could be saved from their deep-rooted ignorance, their "savage" culture, and their bastardized language, which, according to some Portuguese scholars, was a corrupted form of Portuguese "without grammatical rules (they can't even be applied)."[1]

This system could not help but reproduce in children and youth the profile that the colonial ideology itself had created for them, namely that of inferior beings, lacking in all ability.

On the one hand, schooling in these colonies served the purpose of deculturating the natives; on the other hand, it acculturated them into a predefined colonial model. Schools in this mold functioned "as part of an ideological state apparatus designed to secure the ideological and social reproduction of capital and its institutions, whose interests are rooted in the dynamics of capital accumulation and the reproduction of the labor force."[2] This educated labor force in the ex-Portuguese colonies was composed mainly of low-level functionaries whose major tasks were the promotion and maintenance of the status quo. Their role took on a new and important dimension when they were used as intermediaries to further colonize Portuguese possessions in Africa. Thus, colonial schools were successful to the extent that they created a petit-bourgeois class of functionaries who had internalized the belief that they had become "white"

*By African we mean to refer to African natives belonging to African countries that were colonized by Portugal. For the sake of economy of terms, we have selected this term, but we want to point out that we are aware of the great linguistic and cultural diversity that exists in Africa.

or "black with white souls," and were therefore superior to African peasants, who still practiced what was viewed as barbaric culture.

This assimilation process penetrated the deepest level of consciousness, especially in the bourgeois class. For instance, with respect to becoming "white," we are reminded of an anecdote about a black Cape Verdian so preoccupied with his blackness that he paid a well-respected white Cape Verdian to issue him a decree proclaiming him white. The man jokingly wrote for him on a piece of paper "Dja'n branco dja," meaning "I have thereby been declared white."

After independence and in the reconstruction of a new society in these countries, schools have assumed as their major task the "decolonization of mentality," as it is termed by Aristides Pereira, and which Amilcar Cabral called the "re-Africanization of mentality." It is clear that both Pereira and Cabral were well aware of the need to create a school system in which a new mentality cleansed of all vestiges of colonialism would be formulated; a school system that would allow people to appropriate their history, their culture, and their language; a school system in which it was imperative to reformulate the programs of geography, history, and the Portuguese language, changing all the reading texts that were so heavily impregnated with colonialist ideology. It was an absolute priority that students should study their own geography and not that of Portugal, the inlets of the sea and not Rio Tejo. It was urgent that they study their history, the history of the resistance of their people to the invader and the struggle for their liberation, which gave them back the right to make their own history — not the history of the kings of Portugal and the intrigues of the court.

The proposal to incorporate a radical pedagogy in schools has met a lukewarm reception in these countries. We want to argue that the suspicion of many African educators is deeply rooted in the language issue (African versus Portuguese) and has led to the creation of a neocolonialist literacy campaign under the superficially radical slogan of eliminating illiteracy in the new republics. The difficulties of reappropriating African culture have been increased by the fact that the means for such struggle has been the language of the colonizer. As we will argue in this chapter, the present literacy campaign in these nations concerns itself mainly with the creation of functional literates in the Portuguese language. No longer based on the cultural capital of subordinate Africans, the program has fallen prey to positivistic and instrumental approaches to literacy concerned mainly with the mechanical acquisition of Portuguese language skills.[3]

Before our discussion of the politics of an emancipatory literacy program in Africa and elsewhere, we would like to discuss various approaches to literacy. First, we will briefly discuss those approaches derived from a positivistic school and linked to the process of cultural reproduction. Then, we will analyze the role of language in the reproduction process. Finally, we will argue that the only literacy approach that would be consistent with the construction of a new anticolonial society is one rooted in the dynamics of cultural production and informed by a radical pedagogy. That is, the literacy program that is needed is one that will affirm and allow oppressed people to re-create their history, culture, and language; one that will, at the same time, help lead those assimilated individuals who perceive themselves to a be captive to the colonial ideology to "commit class suicide."

APPROACHES TO LITERACY

Almost without exception, traditional approaches to literacy have been deeply ingrained in a positivistic method of inquiry. In effect, this has resulted in an epistemological stance in which scientific rigor and methodological refinement are celebrated, while "theory and knowledge are subordinated to the imperatives of efficiency and technical mastery, and history is reduced to a minor footnote in the priorities of 'empirical' scientific inquiry."[4] In general, this approach abstracts methodological issues from their ideological contexts and consequently ignores the interrelationship between the sociopolitical structures of a society and the act of reading. In part, the exclusion of social and political dimensions from the practice of reading gives rise to an ideology of cultural reproduction, one that views readers as "objects." It is as though their conscious bodies were simply empty, waiting to be filled by that word from the teacher. Although it is important to analyze how ideologies inform various reading traditions, in this chapter we will limit our discussion to a brief analysis of the most important approaches to literacy, linking them to either cultural reproduction or cultural production.

The Academic Approach to Reading

The purpose assigned to reading in the academic tradition is twofold. First, the rationale for this approach "derives from classical definitions of the well-educated man — thoroughly grounded in the classics, articulate in spoken and written expression, actively engaged in intellectual pursuits."[5] This approach to reading has primarily served the interests of the elite classes. In this case, reading is viewed as the acquisition of predefined forms of knowledge and is organized around the study of Latin and Greek and the mastery of the great classical works. Second, since it would be unrealistic to expect the vast majority of society to meet such high standards, reading was redefined as the acquisition of reading skills, decoding skills, vocabulary development, and so on. This second rationale served to legitimize a dual approach to reading: one level for the ruling class and another for the dispossessed majority. According to Giroux (*Theory and Resistance*): "This second notion is geared primarily to working class students whose cultural capital is considered less compatible, and thus inferior in terms of complexity and value, with the knowledge and values of the dominant class."

This twofold academic approach to reading is inherently alienating in nature. On the one hand, it ignores the life experience, the history, and the language practice of students. On the other, it overemphasizes the mastery and understanding of classical literature and the use of literary materials as "vehicles for exercises in comprehension (literal and interpretative), vocabulary development, and word identification skills."[6] Thus, literacy in this sense is stripped of its sociopolitical dimensions; it functions, in fact, to reproduce dominant values and meaning. It does not contribute in any meaningful way to the appropriation of working-class history, culture, and language.

The Utilitarian Approach to Reading

The major goal of the utilitarian approach is to produce readers who meet the basic reading requirements of contemporary society. In spite of its progressive appeal, such an approach emphasizes the mechanical learning of reading skills while sacrificing the critical analysis of the social and political order that generates the need for reading in the first place. This position has led to the development of "functional literates," groomed primarily to meet the requirements of our ever more complex technological society. Such a view is not simply characteristic of the advanced industrialized countries of the West; even within the Third World, utilitarian literacy has been championed as a vehicle for economic betterment, access to jobs, and increase of the productivity level. As it is clearly stated by UNESCO, "Literacy programs should preferably be linked with economic priorities. [They] must impart not only reading and writing, but also professional and technical knowledge, thereby leading to a fuller participation of adults in economic life."[7]

This notion of literacy has been enthusiastically incorporated as a major goal by the back-to-basics proponents of reading. It has also contributed to the development of neatly packaged reading programs that are presented as the solution to difficulties students experience in reading job application forms, tax forms, advertisement literature, sales catalogs, labels, and the like. In general, the utilitarian approach views literacy as meeting the basic reading demand of an industrialized society. As Giroux points out:

> Literacy within this perspective is geared to make adults more productive workers and citizens within a given society. In spite of its appeal to economic mobility, functional literacy reduces the concept of literacy and the pedagogy in which it is suited to the pragmatic requirements of capital; consequently, the notions of critical thinking, culture and power disappear under the imperatives of the labor process and the need for capital accumulation.[8]

Cognitive Development Approach to Reading

While the academic and utilitarian approaches to reading emphasize the mastery of reading skills and view the readers as "objects," the cognitive development model stresses the construction of meaning whereby readers engage in a dialectical interaction between themselves and the objective world. Although the acquisition of literacy skills is viewed as an important task in this approach, the salient feature is how people construct meaning through problem-solving processes. Comprehension of the text is relegated to a position of lesser importance in favor of the development of new cognitive structures that can enable students to move from simple to highly complex reading tasks. This reading process is highly influenced by the early work of John Dewey and has been shaped in terms of the development of Piagetian cognitive structures. Under the cognitive development model, reading is seen as an intellectual process, "through a series of fixed, value-free, and universal stages of development."[9]

The cognitive development model thus avoids criticism of the academic and utilitarian views of reading and fails to consider the content of what is read. Instead, it emphasizes a process that allows students to analyze and critique issues raised in the text with an increasing level of complexity. This approach, however, is rarely concerned with questions of cultural reproduction. Since students' cultural capital — i.e., their life experience, history, and language — is ignored, they are rarely able to engage in thorough critical reflection, regarding their own practical experience and the ends that motivate them in order, in the end, to organize the findings and thus replace mere opinion about facts with an increasingly rigorous understanding of their significance.

The Romantic Approach to Reading

Like the cognitive development model, the romantic approach is based on an interactionist approach with a major focus on the construction of meaning; however, the romantic approach views meaning as being generated by the reader and not occurring in the interaction between reader and author via text. The romantic mode greatly emphasizes the affective and sees reading as the fulfillment of self and a joyful experience. One writer praised "the intimate reliving of fresh views of personality and life implicit in the work (of literature); the pleasure and release of tensions that may flow from such an experience . . . the deepening and broadening of sensitivity to the sensuous quality and emotional impact of day-to-day living."[10]

In essence, the romantic approach to reading presents a counterpoint to the authoritarian modes of pedagogy which view readers as "objects." However, this seemingly liberal approach to literacy fails to make problematic class conflict, gender, or racial inequalities. Furthermore, the romantic model completely ignores the cultural capital of subordinate groups and assumes that all people have the same access to reading, or that reading is part of the cultural capital of all people. This failure to address questions of cultural capital or various structural inequalities means that the romantic model tends to reproduce the cultural capital of the dominant class, to which reading is intimately tied. It is presumptuous and naive to expect a student from the working class, confronted and victimized by myriad disadvantages, to find joy and self-affirmation through reading alone. But more important is the failure of the romantic tradition to link reading to the asymmetrical relations of power within the dominant society, relations of power that not only define and legitimate certain approaches to reading but also disempower certain groups by excluding them from such a process.

We have argued thus far that all of these approaches to literacy have failed to provide a theoretical model for empowering historical agents with the logic of individual and collective self-determination. While these approaches may differ in their basic assumptions about literacy, they all share one common feature: they all ignore the role of language as a major force in the construction of human subjectivities. That is, they ignore the way language may either confirm or deny the life histories and experiences of the people who use it. This becomes clearer in our analysis of the role of language in the literacy programs.

THE ROLE OF LANGUAGE IN LITERACY

In this section we will draw mostly from campaigns in ex-Portuguese African colonies that we directly or indirectly participated in and then followed through their development over the years. Even though we will frequently make reference to these literacy experiments, however, we believe that the issues we raise about the role of language in literacy can be generalized to any linguistic context where there exist asymmetrical power relations.

The literacy programs in ex-Portuguese African colonies have been plagued by constant debate over whether the language of instruction should be the official Portuguese language or the native languages. Such debate, however, hides issues of a more serious nature that are rarely raised. This is in line with Gramsci's argument that: "Each time that in one way or another, the question of language comes to the fore, that signifies that a series of other problems is about to emerge, the formation and enlarging of the ruling class, the necessity to establish more 'intimate' and sure relations between the ruling groups and the national popular masses, that is, the reorganization of cultural hegemony."[11] Gramsci's argument illuminates the issue underlying the debates over language in literacy campaigns we have discussed in this book, debates in which there is still no agreement as to whether the native language is really suited to be a language of instruction. These educators repeatedly use the lack of orthographic uniformity for the African languages to justify their present policy of using Portuguese as the only medium of reading instruction. They raise the question of which dialect such an orthography should be based on. However, the most common argument is that the Portuguese language has international status and therefore guarantees upward mobility for the Portuguese-educated Africans.

The sad reality is that while education in Portuguese provides access to positions of political and economic power for the high echelon of African society, it screens out the majority of the masses, who fail to learn Portuguese well enough to acquire the necessary literacy level for social, economic, and political advancement. By offering a literacy program conducted in the language of the colonizers with the aim of reappropriating the African culture, these educators have, in fact, developed new manipulative strategies that support the maintenance of Portuguese cultural dominance. What is hidden in the language debate in these countries is possibly a resistance to re-Africanization, or perhaps a subtle refusal on the part of the assimilated Africans to "commit class suicide."

The pedagogical and political implications of these literacy programs are far-reaching and yet largely ignored. The reading programs often contradict a fundamental principle of reading, namely that students learn to read faster and with better comprehension when taught in their native tongue. The immediate recognition of familiar words and experiences enhances the development of a positive self-concept in children who are somewhat insecure about the status of their language and culture. For this reason, and to be consistent with the plan to construct a new society in these ex-colonies free from vestiges of colonialism, a literacy program should be based on the rationale that such a program must be rooted in the cultural capital of subordinate Africans and have as its point of departure the native language.

Educators must develop radical pedagogical structures that provide students with the opportunity to use their own reality as a basis of literacy. This includes, obviously, the language they bring to the classroom. To do otherwise is to deny students the rights that lie at the core of the notion of an emancipatory literacy. The failure to base a literacy program on the native language means that oppositional forces can neutralize the efforts of educators and political leaders to achieve decolonization of mind. Educators and political leaders must recognize that "language is inevitably one of the major preoccupations of a society which, liberating itself from colonialism and refusing to be drawn into neo-colonialism, searches for its own recreation. In the struggle to re-create a society, the reconquest by the people of their own world becomes a fundamental factor."[12] It is of tantamount importance that the incorporation of the students' language as the primary language of instruction in literacy be given top priority. It is through their own language that they will be able to reconstruct their history and their culture.

In this sense, the students' language is the only means by which they can develop their own voice, a prerequisite to the development of a positive sense of self-worth. As Giroux elegantly states, the students' voice "is the discursive means to make themselves 'heard' and to define themselves as active authors of their world."[13] The authorship of one's own world, which would also imply one's own language, means what Mikhail Bakhtin defines as "retelling a story in one's own words."

Although the concept of voice is fundamental in the development of an emancipatory literacy, the goal should never be to restrict students to their own vernacular. This linguistic constriction inevitably leads to a linguistic ghetto. Educators must understand fully the broader meaning of student's "empowerment." That is, empowerment should never be limited to what Arnowitz describes as "the process of appreciating and loving oneself."[14] In addition to this process, empowerment should also be a means that enables students "to interrogate and selectively appropriate those aspects of the dominant culture that will provide them with the basis for defining and transforming, rather than merely serving, the wider social order."[15] This means that educators should understand the value of mastering the standard dominant language of the wider society. It is through the full appropriation of the dominant standard language that students find themselves linguistically empowered to engage in dialogue with the various sectors of the wider society. What we would like to reiterate is that educators should never allow the students' voice to be silenced by a distorted legitimation of the standard language. The students' voice should never be sacrificed, since it is the only means through which they make sense of their own experience in the world.

The debate over whether African languages are less suitable as languages of instruction, whether they are restricted or elaborated languages, points to the issue of whether Portuguese is in fact a superior language. In a more important sense, these linguistic categories rest on the technical question of whether African languages are valid and rule-governed systems. Despite synchronic and diachronic analysis of many of these languages, the fact still remains that they continue in a stigmatized and subordinate position. We want to argue that the students' languages have to be understood within the theoretical framework that generates them. Put another way, the ultimate meaning and value of these languages is not to be found by determining how systematic and rule governed they are. We know that already. Their real meaning has to be understood through the assumptions that govern them, and they have to be understood via the social, political, and ideological relations to which they point. Generally speaking, the issue of systematicality and validity often hides the true role of language in the maintenance of the value and interests of the dominant class. In other words, the issue of systematicality and validity becomes a mask that obfuscates questions about social, political, and ideological order within which the subordinate languages exist.

If an emancipatory literacy program is to be developed in the African ex-colonies of Portugal and elsewhere, a program in which readers become "subjects" rather than "objects," educators must understand the productive quality of language. Donald puts it this way:

> I take language to be *productive* rather than *reflective* of social reality. This means calling into question the assumption that we, as speaking subjects, simply use language to organize and express our ideas and experiences. On the contrary, language is one of the most important social practices through which we come to experience ourselves as subjects. My point here is that once we get beyond the idea of language as no more than a medium of communication, as a tool equally and neutrally available to all parties in cultural exchanges, then we can begin to examine language both as a practice of signification and also as a *site* for cultural struggle and as a *mechanism* which produces antagonistic relations between different social groups.[16]

It is to the antagonistic relationship between African and Portuguese speakers that we want to turn now. The potentially antagonistic nature of the African languages has never been fully explored. In order to more clearly discuss this issue of antagonism, we will use Donald's distinction between *oppressed* language and *repressed* language. Using Donald's categories, the "negative" way of posing the language question is to view it in terms of *oppression* — that is, seeing the students' language as "lacking" the dominant language's features, which usually serve as a point of reference for discussion and/or evaluation. By far the most common questions concerning the students' language are posed from the oppression perspective. The alternative view of the students' language is that it is repressed in the dominant standard language. In this view, the subordinate language, as a repressed language, could, if spoken, challenge the privileged linguistic dominance of the standard. Educators have failed to recognize the "positive" promise and antagonistic nature of the subordinate languages. It is precisely on these dimensions that educators must demystify the dominant standard and the old assumptions about its inherent superiority.

Educators must develop an emancipatory literacy program informed by a radical pedagogy so that the students' language will cease to provide its speakers the experience of subordination and, moreover, may be brandished as a weapon of resistance to the dominance of the standard language.

As we stated earlier, the linguistic issues raised in this chapter and throughout this book are not limited to developing countries of Africa and Latin America. The asymmetrical power relations in reference to language use are also predominant in highly industrialized societies. For instance, the U.S. English movement in the United States headed by the ex-California senator S.I. Hayakawa points to a xenophobic culture that blindly negates the pluralistic nature of U.S. society and falsifies the empirical evidence in support of bilingual education, as has been amply documented.[17] These educators, including the present secretary of education, William J. Bennett, fail to understand that it is through multiple discourses that students generate meaning of their everyday social contexts. Without understanding the meaning of their immediate social reality, it is most difficult to comprehend their relations with the wider society.

By and large, U.S. English proponents base their criticism of bilingual education on quantitative evaluation results, which are "the product of a particular model of social structure that gear the theoretical concepts to the pragmatics of the society that devised the evaluation model to begin with."[18] That is, if the results are presented as facts determined by a particular ideological framework, these facts cannot in themselves get us beyond that framework.[19] We would warn educators that these evaluation models can provide answers that are correct and nevertheless without truth. A study that concludes that linguistic minority students in the United States perform way below other mainstream students in English is correct, but such an answer tells us very little about the material conditions with which these linguistic- and racial-minority students work in the struggle against racism, educational tracking, and the systematic negation of their histories.

Bennett's comment that only English "will ensure that local schools will succeed in teaching non-English-speaking students English so that they will [enjoy] access to the opportunities of the American society" points to a pedagogy of exclusion that views the learning of English as education itself. At this point, we would like to raise two fundamental points questions: (1) If English is the most effective educational language, how can we explain that over 60 million Americans are illiterate or functionally illiterate?[20] (2) If education in English *only* can guarantee the linguistic minorities a better future as Bennett promises, why do the majority of black Americans, whose ancestors have been speaking English for over 200 years, find themselves still relegated to the ghettos?

We believe that the answer lies not in the technical questions of whether English is a more elaborate and viable language of instruction. This position would point to an assumption that English is in fact a superior language. We want to propose that the answer rests in a full understanding of the ideological elements that generate and sustain linguistic, racial, and sex discrimination.

Some of these ideological elements are succinctly discussed in Lukas's 1985 analysis of school desegregation in Boston public schools (*Common Ground*). For example, he cites a trip to Charlestown High School, where a group of black parents experienced first-hand the stark reality their children were destined to endure. Although the headmaster assured them that "violence, intimidation, or racial slurs would not be tolerated," they could not avoid the racial epithets on the walls: "Welcome Niggers," "Niggers Suck," "White Power," "KKK," "Bus is for Zulu," and "Be illiterate; fight forced busing." As these parents were boarding the bus, "they were met with jeers and catcalls 'Go home niggers. Keep going all the way to Africa!" This racial intolerance led one parent to reflect, " 'My God, what kind of hell am I sending my children into?'. . . What could her children learn at a school like that except to hate?"[21] Even though forced integration of schools in Boston exacerbated the racial tensions in the Boston public schools, one should not overlook the deep-seated racism that permeates all levels of the school structure. According to Lukas:

Even after Elvira "Prixie" Paladino's election to Boston School Committee she was heard muttering about "jungle bunnies" and "pickaninnes." And John "Bigga" Kerrigan, [also elected to the School Committee] prided himself on the unrestrained invective ("I may be a prick, but at least I'm a consistent prick"), particularly directed at blacks ("savages") and the liberal media ("mother-fucking maggots") and Lem Tucker, a black correspondent for ABC News, whom Kerrigan described as "one generation away from swinging in the trees," a remark he illustrated by assuming his hands upwards, and scratching his armpits.[22]

Against this landscape of violent racism perpetrated against racial minorities, and also against linguistic minorities, one can understand the reasons for the high dropout rate in the Boston public schools (approximately 50 percent). Perhaps racism and other ideological elements are part of a school reality which forces a high percentage of students to leave school, only later to be profiled by the very system as dropouts or "poor and unmotivated students."

EMANCIPATORY LITERACY

In maintaining a certain coherence with the revolutionary plan to reconstruct new and more democratic societies, educators and political leaders need to create a new school grounded in a new educational praxis, expressing different concepts of education consonant with the plan for the society as a whole. In order for this to happen, the first step is to identify the objectives of the inherited dominant education. Next, it is necessary to analyze how the methods used by the dominant schools function, legitimize the dominant values and meanings, and at the same time negate the history, culture, and language practices of the majority of subordinate students. The new school, so it is argued, must also be informed by a radical pedagogy, which would make concrete such values as solidarity, social responsibility, creativity, discipline in the service of the common good, vigilance, and critical spirit. An important feature of a new educational plan is the development of literacy programs rooted in an emancipatory ideology, where readers become "subjects" rather than mere "objects." The new literacy program needs to move away from traditional approaches, which emphasize the acquisition of mechanical skills while divorcing reading from its ideological and historical contexts. In attempting to meet this goal, it purposely must reject the conservative principles embedded in the approaches to literacy we have discussed earlier. Unfortunately, many new literacy programs sometimes unknowingly reproduce one common feature of those approaches by ignoring the important relationship between language and the cultural capital of the people at whom the literacy program was aimed. The result is the development of a literacy campaign whose basic assumptions are at odds with the revolutionary spirit that launched it.

The new literacy programs must be largely based on the notion of emancipatory literacy, in which literacy is viewed "as one of the major vehicles by which 'oppressed' people are able to participate in the sociohistorical transformation of their society."[23] In this view, literacy programs should be tied not only to mechanical learning of reading skills but, additionally, to a critical understanding of the overall goals for national reconstruction. Thus, the reader's development of a critical comprehension of the text, and the sociohistorical context to which it refers, becomes an important factor in our notion of literacy. The act of learning to read and write, in this instance, is a creative act that involves a critical comprehension of reality. The knowledge of earlier knowledge, gained by the learners as a result of analyzing praxis in its social context, opens to them the possibility of a new knowledge. The new knowledge reveals the reason for being that is behind the facts, thus demythologizing the false interpretations of these same facts. Thus, there is no longer any separation between thought-language and objective reality. The reading of a text now demands a reading within the social context to which it refers.

Literacy, in this sense, is grounded in a critical reflection on the cultural capital of the oppressed. It becomes a vehicle by which the oppressed are equipped with the necessary tools to reappropriate their history, culture, and language practices. It is, thus, a way to enable the oppressed to reclaim "those historical and existential experiences that are devalued in everyday life by the dominant culture in order to be both validated and critically understood."[24]

The theories underlying emancipatory literacy have been, in principle, wholeheartedly embraced by many educators in many parts of the world, particularly in Latin America and the ex-Portuguese colonies in Africa. However, we must argue that, in practice, the assimilated middle class, especially teachers trained by the colonial schools, has not been fully able to play a radical pedagogical role. These educators sometimes fail to analyze and understand the ways in which the ruling class uses the dominant language to maintain class division, thereby keeping subordinate people in their proper place. For example, we are reminded of a friend in Cape Verde who, having intellectually embraced the revolutionary cause, is unable to perceive himself as still being emotionally "captive" to the colonial ideology. But when we asked him which language he most often uses in the office, he quickly answered, "Portuguese, of course. It is the only way to keep my subordinates in their place. If I speak Cape Verdian, they don't respect me."

This view of language in Cape Verde is illustrative of the extent to which Cape Verdians are held "captive" by the dominant ideology, which devalues their own language. Not surprisingly, many progressive educators and leaders fail to recognize and understand the importance of their native language in the development of an emancipatory literacy. As we mentioned before, literacy programs in the ex-colonies of Portugal are conducted in Portuguese, the language of the colonizer. The same is true for industrialized nations such as the United States, where the language of instruction is always the standard language at the sacrifice of minority and less prestigious languages. The continued use of the dominant standard language as a vehicle of literacy will only guarantee that future leaders will be the sons and daughters of the ruling class.

In essence, progressive educators sometimes not only fail to recognize the positive promise of the students' language, but they systematically undermine the principles of an emancipatory literacy by conducting literacy programs in the standard language of the dominant class. The result is that the learning of reading skills in the dominant standard language will not enable subordinate students to acquire the critical tools "to awaken and liberate them from their mystified and distorted view of themselves and their world."[25] Educators must understand the all-encompassing role the dominant language has played in this mystification and distortion process. They must also recognize the antagonistic nature of the subordinate language and its potential challenge to the mystification of dominant language superiority. Finally, they must develop a literacy program based on the theory of cultural production. In other words, subordinate students must become *actors* in the reconstruction process of a new society.

Literacy can only be emancipatory and critical to the extent that it is conducted in the language of the people. It is through the native language that students "name their world" and begin to establish a dialectical relationship with the dominant class in the process of transforming the social and political structures that imprison them in their "culture of silence." Thus, a person is literate to the extent that he or she is able to use language for social and political reconstruction.[26] The use of the dominant language only in literacy programs weakens the possibilities for subordinate students to engage in dialectical encounters with the dominant class. Literacy conducted in the dominant standard language empowers the ruling class by sustaining the status quo. It supports the maintenance of the elitist model of education. This elite model of education creates intellectualists and technocrats rather then intellectuals and technicians. In short, literacy conducted in the dominant language is alienating to subordinate students, since it denies them the fundamental tools for reflection, critical thinking, and social interaction. Without the cultivation of their native language, and robbed of the opportunity for reflection and critical thinking, subordinate students find themselves unable to re-create their culture and history. Without the reappropriation of their cultural capital, the reconstruction of the new society envisioned by progressive educators and leaders can hardly be a reality.

Appendix

Letter to Mario Cabral

July 15, 1977

Geneva

Dear Comrade Mario Cabral,

From the moment we began our dialogue in the first letters that I wrote you (a dialogue that not only continually grew more profound, but that also has been extended to other comrades), a constant worry accompanied us: would we be seen as "international experts" in our collaboration with Guinea and Cape Verde or as actual militants? As comrades, could we involve ourselves more and more in the common effort of national reconstruction? For us the type of collaboration in which we individually and as a team functioned in a dispassionate way as "technical consultants" would have been impossible. So it is, also, that you understood, from the beginning, our presence there. What you wanted and expected from us was what we were seeking to do and to be.

If this coagreement had not been ongoing, we could have been regarded as impertinent. At one or another moment of our common work what always moved us was and continues to be our spirit of militancy.

It is with this same spirit that I write you one more letter. A letter that, although written and signed by me, summarizes the position of the whole team and constitutes a kind of report, albeit incomplete, concerning our last meeting in Geneva, the meeting in which we tried to achieve a critical balance of the activities that have so closely connected us to Guinea-Bissau.

We may remember, as a didactic exercise, some of the points that the Commission of Education and we together saw as fundamental points, right from the start of our activities:

1. That the literacy of adults, like all education, is a political act, unable for this reason to be reduced to the purely mechanical learning of reading and writing.

2. That the learning of the reading and writing of texts, in line with the political stance of the PAIGC (with which we agree) implies a critical understanding of the social context to which the texts refer: it demands the "reading" of reality by those becoming literate through the analysis of the social practice, whose productive act is a basic dimension. Thus it is impossible to separate literacy and education in general from production and, by necessity, extension from health.

3. That the introduction of the written word in areas where the social memory is exclusively or predominantly oral presupposes infrastructural transformations capable of making written communication necessary. Thus, there was a need to establish the areas of priority for literacy, that is, those areas that were suffering from transformation or were suffering from them for a short time.

Taking these items as a field of reference for the analysis of what it was possible to do this year, as well as a few experiences from which we have all learned, it has become obvious that the central point and the major problem to be reflected upon and discussed is that of language.

On several occasions, we discussed the question of language in our letters and in our work meetings. If I am not mistaken, we debated about language in the very heart of the National Commission, in its inaugural session, and once more in its last meeting. We often dealt with this problem with members of the Coordinating Commission, returning to it there in one of the study meetings over which you presided last June and in which Mario de Andrade participated, together with comrades from other sectors of the Commission on Education. This was the meeting in which Marcos Arruda [a member of the IDAC team at that time] proposed some relevant suggestions in a small text. And finally, I can still quote the last conversation that we had with the Comrade President, whose main focus was language.

A little over a year ago, if we are interpreting the government policies correctly, it was believed that literacy in the Portuguese language would be viable, recognizing Creole as the national language. The radical reason for literacy in the foreign language was the continual lack of a written discipline for Creole. It was believed that as long as this discipline was not achieved, there was no reason to leave the People illiterate. The very results that were being realized with the literacy program in Portuguese, in the heart of the FARP, reinforced this hypothesis.

Nevertheless, what our practice is demonstrating is that learning the Portuguese language obviously works, although with difficulties, in cases in which Portuguese is found not to be totally foreign to the social practice of those becoming literate. This is exactly the case of the FARP, like that of certain sectors of activities of urban centers such as Bissau. But this is not the situation in the rural centers of the country, where one finds the oppressed majority of the national population, and in whose social practice the Portuguese language does not exist. In truth, the Portuguese language is not the language of the People of Guinea-Bissau. It is not by chance that the Comrade President becomes tired, as he confessed to us, when he must speak in Portuguese for a long period of time.

What is being observed in the rural zones, in spite of the high level of interest and motivation of those becoming literate and of the cultural facilitators, is that it is impossible to learn a foreign language as if it were a national language. As a virtually unknown language, during the centuries of colonial pressure, the people fought to preserve their cultural identity, resisting being "touched" by the dominant language, even as they were being "helped" by the way in which the colonizers behaved toward the organization of the productive forces of the country. The use of their native languages was, for a long time, one of the only means of resistance available to the people. It is not strange, then, that the cultural facilitators in these same areas have precariously dominated means of using Portuguese. What does seem strange is that under such circumstances, there is some actual learning of the Portuguese language.

For example, if there is any area where the literacy effort was expected to produce the best results, this would be the Co. The Maximo Gorki Center, integrating itself more and more into the life of the communities around it, and counting on effective professors and apprentices with a high level of political consciousness, had all the necessary conditions to become a nucleus of support for literacy efforts.

Nevertheless, what was observed through experience and confirmed last June with Augusta's and Marcos Arruda's evaluation is that those who were becoming literate, after the long months of work, were only taking "a tiring walk" around generative words. They marched on from the first to the fifth; by the fifth, they had forgotten the third. They returned to the third and perceived that they had forgotten the first and the second. On the other hand, upon trying to create words with the syllabic combination available to them, they rarely did it in Portuguese.

I myself had the opportunity to see words written by some of them whose writing coincided with that of Portuguese words, but whose meaning was altogether different, since they were thinking about *mancanha*. Why? Because the Portuguese language has nothing to do with their social practice. In their everyday experience, there is not a single moment in which the Portuguese language is necessary. Nor is it necessary in conversations with family, in encounters with neighbors, in productive work, in purchases in the market, in traditional parties, in hearing the Comrade President, or in memories of the past. In the latter case, what should be clear is that the Portuguese language is the language of the *tugas* [Portuguese colonialists], from which they defended themselves throughout the entire colonial period.

One could argue that this difficulty in learning is due to the lack of support materials. Nevertheless, it seems purely secondary to us that the lack of these materials, in the broadest possible sense, could be the principal cause. What I mean to say is that, even taking advantage of good support material, as we will have in the Popular Education Notebook, the results would be only a little better. It is just that the Notebook, while it is support material in and of itself, is not capable of overcoming the fundamental, substantial reason for the difficulty: the absence of the Portuguese language in the social practice of the People. Nor is foreign language — Portuguese — a part of the social practice of the great masses of the oppressed of Guinea-Bissau. It is not imposed at any of the levels of their daily practice, at the level of the fight for production, at that of the conflicts of interest, at that of the creative activity of the People. The learning of a foreign language imposes itself as a necessity on people or on social groups when, at least on one of these levels, this learning becomes important.

To insist, then, in our case, on the teaching of Portuguese, means to impose on the population a useless and impossible task. It would not be too much, in fact, it would be absolutely indispensable to extend these thoughts about language a little further into the framework of the national reconstruction and creation of a new society in which the exploitation of one over another is eliminated (commensurate with the major ideals that always inspired the PAIGC). The PAIGC went about forging these ideals as the authentic vanguard of the People of Guinea and Cape Verde.

Although Portuguese calls itself merely the official language, with the prerogative, in doing so, of being the national language (since it is through its use that it becomes a substantial part of the intellectual formation of children and youths), its prolonged retention will work against the concretization of those ideals.

Let us emphasize that we do not mean to say that the Party and the Government should have suspended all the systematic educational activities of the country that did not rely on written Creole. This is so absurd as to be inconceivable. Indeed, we may say emphatically that the urgency of such a discipline will make the Creole language a viable national language in concrete terms, which in turn will cause Portuguese to assume, little by little, its real stature in the educational system of the country — that of a foreign language, and to be taught as such.

On the contrary, to the extent that Portuguese continues to be the language in the educational system that mediates a great part of the intellectual formation of those becoming educated, a real democratization of this formation will be rather difficult, in spite of the undeniable efforts now going on. The Portuguese language will come to establish a social division in the country, creating a small, privileged urban minority, as opposed to the oppressed majority of the populace. Undoubtedly it will be easier for that minority, with access to Portuguese by their very social position, to take advantage of the majority in the acquisition of a certain type of knowledge in written as well as oral expression. This access to Portuguese will satisfy one of the requirements for the minority's advancement in studies, with X number of consequences that can be foreseen.

How does one reply to this challenge, above all when one relies on an advantage that is not always there, that is, the presence of a language of national unity such as Creole? What policy of action could we adopt, suitable to the concrete data of this reality? Not pretending to respond to these questions' full complexity, questions that involve the cultural and educational policy of the country, we limit ourselves merely to some suggestions, by way of our humble collaboration as comrades.

First, we believe it urgent to concretize that which you and Mario de Andrade are considering, to which I referred above: that is, the written discipline of Creole, with the assistance of linguists who are equally militant.

While this work on the discipline of Creole was being done, we would limit, in the field of cultural action, the literacy program in Portuguese:

1. To the area of Bissau, where the population, mastering the Creole language perfectly, is familiar with Portuguese. There, above all, literacy in Portuguese would be done on the work fronts, in which reading and writing this language could mean something important to those who are learning and to the effort of national reconstruction.

2. To certain rural areas, when and if the programs of socio-economic development demand technical abilities from the workers, which, in turn, demand the reading and writing of Portuguese. In this case, if Creole is not spoken fluently, as it is in Bissau, one may still impose a reinvestigation of the

methodology to be used for the teaching of the Portuguese language.

In all of these cases, nevertheless, it would be indispensable to discuss with those becoming literate the reasons that lead us to actualize literacy in Portuguese.

Thus, one can perceive how limited action in the sector of adult literacy would be. And what do we do with respect to the populations that are not found in the above areas? Engage them, little by little, in view of the limitations of people and of material, in a serious effort of animation or cultural action. Engage them, in other words, in the "reading," in the "rereading," and the "writing" of reality, without the reading and writing of words.

While cultural action is political-pedagogical action that includes literacy, it is not always forced to revolve around literacy. Many times it is possible, and more than possible, it is necessary to work with communities in the "reading" of their reality. It is necessary to relate projects of action, such as collective vegetable gardens, cooperatives of production, with efforts of health education (without, however, necessarily asking the populace to read words). From this we can affirm that if all learning of reading and writing of words necessarily presupposes the reading and writing of reality, in a political vision such as that of the PAIGC and ourselves (that is, the involvement of the populace in projects of action over reality), not all programs of action over reality initially imply the learning the reading and writing of words.

Aiming at the mobilization of the masses, aiming at their organization so that they may engage in projects of transformational action, of their milieu, cultural action should begin with a precise knowledge of the conditions of this content; likewise it should be sincerely of a knowledge of the needs felt by the people, as the people's need to be more profound is not always readily perceived and clearly delineated.

The "reading" of reality, centered on the critical understanding of social practice, allows the people this clarification. It was not by accident that a Sedengalese participant in one excellent program of cultural action (either of cultural facilitation or popular education, it doesn't really matter what one calls it) affirmed: "Before, we did not know what we knew. Now, we know that we did know and that we can know more."

Upon making the affirmation, it seems beyond doubt that this comrade, who is taking possession of a critical understanding of what knowledge is, and whence its source, was not referring to the precarious domination that was being painfully exercised over one or another generative word in Portuguese. Indeed, he was referring to the dimensions of reality that he and others were discovering, in the productive work, in the collective gardens.

At the moment, one of the problems posed in the specific case of Sedengal is the concrete reply to the last part of that comrade's discourse, expressing not only his level of curiosity but also that of the others. That is, how do we reply, translated in terms of action and reflection, to what he says so clearly: "Now we know that we can know more." What is imposed is the definition of what might constitute the "universe" of knowledge in the "now we know that we can know more": in other words, to define what one can know more about.

One may observe, on the other hand, the undeniable level of theoretical abstraction expressed in the discourse, independently of its author not being literate. He departs from the affirmation that "before they did not know that they knew." While engaged in production of a collective nature, upon discovering what they knew, he correctly infers "that they now can know more," even though it may not define the object to be known.

There is no doubt that it would be interesting if efforts of cultural action like that of Sedengal (to name only one) could already include literacy in their success. Independent of this, Sedengal affirms itself today more and more on the national level in Guinea-Bissau. And it is affirmed not because the participants of the Culture Circles had come to be able to write and read short sentences in the Portuguese language. Rather it is because, at a certain moment in the impossible learning of that language, they discovered what was possible: collective work. And it was through this form of work, in which they began to rewrite and reread their reality, that they touched and awakened the entire community. By all indications, they will be able to turn Sedengal into a real example.

No text, no more correct and flowing a reading, could have been presented in the closing of the first phase of activities of the Culture Circles of Sedengal (in which comrade Mario Cabral participated) and the collective garden than the active presence of a population engaged in the job of national reconstruction. Sedengal is already a concrete example of the multitude of things that can be done in a country by means of cultural action without literacy; it is a very rich source of learning and the possibility of new tableaus.

It seems to us that, in Co, where highly favorable conditions are found, as is commonly known, one could attempt a second front of cultural action, integrating health with agriculture, using health as a point of departure. For this reason, we would try to develop a manual about health education, directed to those becoming animated and containing the most elementary notions about how a community, through collective work and transformation of its environment, can better its health and prevent illness.

A preproject to this manual, elaborated here along these general lines, would be taken to Bissau in September, where, if our project is accepted, it would be reviewed by the national specialists and mimeographed immediately. In October, the training of the facilitators would be done and the program would begin.

To be well received and continuously evaluated, the development of the experience would serve to perfect the education of the facilitators, to test and improve the manual and challenge the creativity of everyone, with respect to the creation of new support materials, as well as new forms of language that reflect reality, so that communication is carried out more efficiently.

If we were dealing with an area whose population was found from a political point of view to be in the beginning stages, we would have another starting procedure. We all know, however, that the Committee of the Party is representing the action of the Maximo Gorki Center together with the populations of the *tabancas* [tribal huts] of Co, and their interaction.

In this way, on one hand, we would have Sedengal moving, developing new programmatic contents of cultural action, with the ever-growing collaboration of the Commission on Agriculture, joining the Commission on Health. On the other hand, the project of Co and the two commissions are defining themselves as sources of experience and dynamic centers to enable the realization of tableaus and to work in programs of other areas, as we said earlier.

Broadly speaking, these are, friend and comrade Mario Cabral, the considerations that we send to you, one month before Miguel, Rosiska, and Claudius go there.

With a fraternal hug from Elza and me and the entire team, to comrade Beatriz and you.

Paulo Freire

Chapter Notes

Foreword

1. In these comments, I have included remarks from my introduction of Paulo Freire at the Kennedy Library in Boston in 1985 and have incorporated passages from a report on Paulo Freire's visit to the University of Massachussetts at Boston in 1984, prepared at the request of James H. Broderick and published by him for distribution to the Faculty of Arts and Sciences. Freire's visit was sponsored by Scholarship in Teaching, a program directed by Professor Broderick and funded by the Ford Foundation. In preparing this introduction, I have consulted my friends and colleagues Elsa Auerbach, Lil Brannon, Neal Bruss, Louise Dunlap, and Dixie Goswami.

2. A fellow admirer of Paulo Freire once scolded me for speaking of a "pedagogy of knowing" rather than of "Freire's 'pedagogy of the oppressed.'" They are one and the same: the pedagogy of the oppressed, if it is not to be on banking or nutrition models, must be "a pedagogy of knowing," a phrase Freire employs in his important essay on conscientization. See *The Politics of Education*, trans. Donaldo Macedo (South Hadley, Mass.: Bergin and Garvey, 1985) p. 55.

3. I have put *discourse* in quotation marks not because I think

it is unreal or superficial but as a way of signaling the problematic character of the term. In literary study, *discourse* is nonspecific; furthermore a poetic *discourse* is "nondiscursive" in the sense that its abstractions take a different form from those found in argumentation and other kinds of exposition. In sociolinguistics, *discourse* is generally defined in terms of its relationship to work ("production"). In psycholinguistics, *discourse* is the object of stylistic analysis with pretensions to wider significance.

Careless use of the term tends to institutionalize what is a pseudo-concept, in Vygotsky's sense. It is especially dangerous insofar as it can seem to legitimate the vague conceptions of B. L. Whorf's "linguistic relativity." What is crucial to remember is that *discourse* is not synonymous with *language* and that it is formed and shaped by culture, as the formal structure of language is not. I have explored this matter in "Sapir and the Two Tasks of Language," forthcoming in *Semiotica*.

4. Ann Berthoff, Angela Dorenkamp, and Jean Lind-Brenkman followed this form at the Conference on College Composition and Communication (1980). The panel topic was "The Political Implications of Research in Composition."

5. James Reither (Department of English, St. Thomas University, Fredericton, New Brunswick, E3B 5G3 Canada) is the editor of *Inkshed*, a newsletter intended "to intensify relationships among research, theory, and practice relating to language, language acquisition, and language-use." *Inkshed* is supported by St. Thomas University and the voluntary contributions of subscribers.

Introduction

1. Antonio Gramsci, quoted in James Donald, "Language, Literacy, and Schooling," in *The State and Popular Culture*, (Milton Keynes: Open University, U203 Popular Culture Unit, 1982), p. 44. For Gramsci's remarks on language, see Antonio Gramsci, *The Modern Prince and Other Writings*, trans. by Louis Marks, (New York: New World Paperbacks, 1957), passim; *Selections from the Prison Notebooks*, eds. Q. Hoare and G. Nowell Smith (New York: International Publishers, 1971); and *Letters from Prison* (London: Jonathan Cape, 1975).

2. See, for example, Paulo Freire, *Pedagogy of the Oppressed* (New York: Seabury Press, 1970); Paulo Freire, *Education for Critical Consciousness* (New York: Seabury Press, 1973); Paulo Freire, *The Politics of Education* (South Hadley, Mass.: Bergin and Garvey, 1985); Mikhail Bakhtin, *The Dialogic Imagination*, trans. by Caryl Emerson and Michael Holquist (Austin: University of Texas, 1981); V. N. Volosinov [M.M. Bakhtin], *Marxism and the Philosophy of Language* (New York: Seminar Press, 1973); and V. N. Volosinov [M.M. Bakhtin], *Freudianism: A Marxist Critique* (New York: Academic Press, 1976).

3. For a classic advocacy statement of this position, see Research and Policy Committee of the Committee for Economic Development, *Investing in Our Children: Business and the Public Schools* (New York: Committee for Economic Development, 1985). A critique of this position can be found in Stanley Aronowitz and Henry A. Giroux, *Education Under Siege* (South Hadley, Mass.: Bergin and Garvey, 1985).

4. This is particularly obvious not only in the discourse of cultural deprivation theorists of the new right such as Nathan Glazer, but also a matter of federal policy on education. For instance, Secretary of Education William Bennett, an outspoken opponent of bilingualism, argues a position that is less an attack on language-minority policy *per se* than it is on the role that education might play in the empowerment of minorities by dignifying their culture and experience. For an interesting popular analysis of this issue, see James Crawford, "Bilingual Educators Discuss Politics of Education," *Education Week* (November 19, 1986), pp. 15–16. For a more theoretical treatment, see James Cummins, "Empowering Minority Students: A Framework for Intervention," *Harvard Educational Review* 56 (February 1986), pp. 18–36.

5. Stanley Aronowitz, "Why Should Johnny Read?" *The Village Voice Literary Supplement* (May 1985), p. 13.

6. For an exception to this issue, see the various articles on the politics of literacy, edited by Donald Lazere, in *Humanities in Society* 4 (Fall 1981). See also Richard Ohmann, *English in America* (Cambridge and Oxford: Oxford University Press, 1976); Richard Ohmann, "Literacy, Technology, and Monopoly Cap-

ital," *College English* 47 (1985), pp. 675–84; Valerie Miller, *Between Struggle and Hope: The Nicaraguan Literacy Crusade* (Boulder: West-view Press, 1985); Aronowitz, "Why Should Johnny Read?" and Donald, "Language, Literature, and Schooling." For a review of the conservative, liberal, and radical literature on literacy, see Henry A. Giroux, *Theory and Resistance in Education* (South Hadley, Mass.: Bergin and Garvey, 1983); Linda Brodkey, "Tropics of Literacy," *Boston University Journal of Education* 168 (1986), pp. 47–54; Rita Roth, "Schooling, Literacy Acquisition, and Cultural Transmission," *Boston University Journal of Education* 166 (1984), pp. 291–308; and Ira Shor, *Culture Wars* (New York: Routledge and Kegan Paul, 1986). For an excellent demonstration of the relationship between a radical theory of literacy and classroom practice, see Alex McLeod, "Critical Literacy: Taking Control of Our Own Lives," *Language Arts* 63 (January 1986), pp. 37–50, and Shirley Heath, *Way With Words* (New York: McGraw Hill, 1983). For an excellent review of the literature on literacy and reading instruction, see Patrick Shannon, "Reading Instruction and Social Class," *Language Arts* 62 (October 1985), pp. 604–11; and for an important critique of the dominant approach to reading and literacy based on the use of Basal Readers, see Kenneth Goodman, "Basal Readers: A Call for Action," *Language Arts* 63 (April 1986), pp. 358–63.

7. For a superb theoretical analysis of the relationship between Freire's work and the discourse of hope and transformation, see Peter McLaren, "Postmodernity and the Death of Politics: A Brazilian Reprieve," *Educational Theory* 36 (1986), pp. 389–401.

8. For a more recent view of Freire's theory of literacy and politics, see David Dillon, "Reading the World and Reading the Word: An Interview with Paulo Freire," *Language Arts* 62 (January 1985), pp. 15–21.

9. Antonio Gramsci, *Selection from Prison Notebooks*, eds. and trans. Quinten Hoare and Geoffrey Smith (New York: International Publishers, 1971).

10. For an outstanding discussion of literacy and ideology, see Linda Brodkey, *Writing on Parole: Essays and Studies on Academic Discourse* (Philadelphia: Temple University, forthcoming).

11. Aronowitz and Giroux, *Education Under Siege*.

12. Gillian Swanson, "Rethinking Representations," *Screen* 27 (October 1986), pp. 16–28.

13. Roger Simon, "Empowerment as a Pedagogy of Possibility," *Language Arts* (forthcoming).

14. Stanley Aronowitz, "Why Should Johnny Read?"

15. Philip Corrigan, "State Formation and Classroom Practice," paper delivered at the Ivor Goodson Seminar, University of Western Ontario, 2–3 October 1986.

16. For a critical discussion of theories of reproduction and resistance, see Henry A. Giroux, *Theory and Resistance in Education*; also see J. C. Walker, "Romanticising Resistance, Romanticising Culture: Problems in Willis's Theory of Cultural Production," *British Journal of Sociology of Education* 7:1 (1986), pp. 59–80.

17. Fred Inglis, *The Management of Ignorance* (London: Blackwell 1985), p. 108.

18. Harold Rosen, "The Importance of Story," *Language Arts* 63 (March 1986), pp. 226–37.

19. Walter Benjamin, *Illuminations*, ed. Hannah Arendt (New York: Schocken, 1969), especially "Thesis on the Philosophy of History," pp. 253–64.

20. Ernst Bloch, *The Principle of Hope*, III (Cambridge: Mass.: MIT, 1985). For a discussion of the politics of antiutopianism, hope, and struggle in radical theories of education, see Henry A. Giroux, "Solidarity, Struggle, and the Public Sphere, parts 1 & 2," *The Review of Education* (forthcoming).

21. This theme is most developed in the various works and traditions of liberation theology. For an insightful overview and critical analysis of this perspective, see Rebecca S. Chopp, *The Praxis of Suffering* (Maryknoll, N.Y.: Orbis, 1986).

22. See Herbert Marcuse, *Eros and Civilization* (Boston: Beacon, 1955), and Paul Ricoeur, *Freud and Philosophy: An Essay on Interpretation*, trans. Denis Savage (New Haven: Yale University, 1970).

23. Martin Jay, "Anamnestic Totalization," *Theory and Society* 11 (1982), p. 13.

24. Peter McLaren, *Schooling as a Ritual Performance* (New York: Routledge and Kegan Paul, 1986).

25. Simon, "Empowerment", p. 4

26. David Lusted, "Why Pedagogy?" *Screen* 27 (September–October 1986), pp. 4–5.

27. For an important analysis of similar issues, see Kathleen Weiler, *Women Teaching for Change* (South Hadley, Mass.: Bergin and Garvey, 1987).

28. For a superb history of curriculum as a field of struggle, see Herbert M. Kliebard, *The Struggle for the American Curriculum 1893–1958* (New York: Routledge and Kegan Paul, 1986).

29. Henry A. Giroux, "Radical Pedagogy and the Politics of Student Voice," *Interchange* 17 (1986), pp. 48–69.

30. Sharon Welch, *Communities of Resistance and Solidarity* (New York: Orbis, 1985).

31. Simon, "Empowerment", pp. 11–12.

32. Swanson, "Rethinking Representations."

33. Dieter Misgeld, "Education and Cultural Invasion: Critical Social Theory, Education as Instruction, and the 'Pedagogy of the Oppressed,' " in *Critical Theory and Public Life*, ed. John Forester (Cambridge, Mass.: MIT, 1985), pp. 106–7.

34. Michelle Fine, "Silencing in Public Schools," *Language Arts* 64 (1987), pp. 157–74.

35. This issue is well developed in Michelle Sola and Adrian T. Bennett, "The Struggle for Voice: Narrative, Literacy, and Consciousness in an East Harlem School," *Boston University Journal of Education* 167 (1985), pp. 88–110.

36. Samuel Bowles and Herbert Gintis, *Schooling in Capitalist Society* (New York: Basic Books, 1976) and Paul Willis, *Learning to Labor* (New York: Columbia University, 1981).

37. Aronowitz and Giroux, *Education Under Siege*, especially chapter 2, pp. 23–46.

38. Sara Freedman, Jane Jackson, and Katherine Boles, "The Other End of the Corridor: The Effect of Teaching on Teachers," *Radical Teacher* No. 23 (1983), pp. 2–23.

Chapter 1

1. An earlier version of this chapter was first published in the *Boston University Journal of Education*, Vol. no. 165 (1983). It was originally translated by Loretta Slover.

Chapter 2

1. Paulo Freire, "A Alfabetização de Adultos — Crítica de sua visão ingenua, compreensão de sua visão crítica," in *Ação Cultural para a Liberdade e Outros Escritos*, 5th ed. (Rio de Janeiro: Paz e Terra, 1981).

2. Relevant to naive and astute people, see Paulo Freire, "O Papel educativo das igrejas na América Latina," in *Ação Cultural para a Liberdade e Outros Escritos*, p. 15.

3. See Paulo Freire, *Cartas a Guiné-Bissau* (Rio de Janeiro: Paz e Terra).

4. See Paulo Freire, *Pedagogia do Oprimido* (Rio de Janeiro: Paz e Terra); and "Criando Métodos de Pesquisa Alternativa — Aprendendo a Fazê-la Através da Ação," in Carlos Rodrigues Brandão, ed., *Pesquisa Participante* (São Paulo: Editora Brasiliense, 1981).

Chapter 3

1. Richard Johnson, "What Is Cultural Studies Anyway?" *Angistica* 26, nos. 1, 2 (1983).

Chapter 4

1. For a detailed analysis of both these Notebooks, especially the first, which is not discussed in this text, see Paulo Freire, "Quatro Cartas aos Animadores de Círculos de Cultura de São Tomé e Príncipe," in Carlos Brandão, ed. *A Questão Politica da Educacao Popular* (São Paulo: Editora Brasiliense, 1980).

2. See the excellent article by D. Merril Swert, "Proverbs, Parables and Metaphors — Applying Freire's Concept of Codification to Africa," in *Convergence* 14, no. 1 (1981).

3. On how to work with this Notebook, again see Freire, "Quatro Cartas."

4. This disdain toward oneself tends to be overcome by a feeling of assurance and self-confidence, to the extent that large popular sectors, mobilizing themselves around claims that are fundamental to them, organize themselves to concretize them. Then they can begin knowing and demanding to know more.

5. "In any physical work, although it may be the most mechanical and lowly, there always exists a minimum of technical

quality, or rather, a minimum of creative intellectual activity."
Antonio Gramsci, *Cuadernos de la Cárcel: Los intelectuales y las
organizació de la cultura* (México D.F.: Juan Pablos Editor, 1975),
p. 14.

6. Antonio Gramsci, quoted by Angelo Broccoli, in *Antonio
Gramsci y la Educación como Hegemonía* (Mexico: Editorial Nueva
Imagen S.A., 1979), p. 47.

7. The reading and discussion of this text in one of the grad-
uate courses that I coordinate at the PUO provoked interesting
analyses and observations on the part of the participants. "One
should never lose sight," said Cristiano Amaral Giorgi, "of
something essential for the educational objective: that the initial
point of discussion may be the work such as it is in fact perceived
and interpreted by the group of workers involved in the process.
In this way, the idea of human transformation, in the transforming of nature through work, is perceived by the rural
worker as clearly consistent with what he sees of his action. The
perception of the urban worker, especially of the tertiary sector,
is not necessarily the same. The discussion should, in this case,
be presented in new terms, including a series of other
mediations."

8. The verbs were studied at the beginning of the Notebook.

Chapter 7

1. J. Caetano, *Boletim da Sociedade de Geografia* (Lisbon, n.d.),
p. 349.

2. H. A. Giroux, *Theory and Resistance: A Pedagogy for Opposition* (South Hadley, Mass.: J.F. Bergin Pub., 1983), p. 87

3. P. Bourdieu and J. C. Passeron, *Reproduction in Education,
Society, and Culture* (Beverly Hills, Calif.: Sage, 1977).

4. Giroux, *Theory and Resistance.*

5. S. Walmsley, "On the Purpose and Content of Secondary
Reading Programs," *Curriculum Inquiry* 11 (1981), p. 78.

6. Ibid., p. 80.

7. UNESCO, *An Asian Model of Educational Development*
(Paris: UNESCO, 1966), p. 97.

8. Giroux, *Theory and Resistance.*

9. Walmsley, "Purpose and Content," p. 82.

10. L. Rosenblatt, "The Enriching Values of Reading," in *Reading in an Age of Mass Communication*, ed. William S. Gray (New York: Appleton-Century Crofts, 1949), pp. 37-38.

11. Antonio Gramsci, cited in J. Donald, *Language, Literacy and Schooling* (London: Open University Press, in press).

12. J. Kenneth, "The Sociology of Pierre Bourdieu," *Educational Review* 25 (1973).

13. H. A. Giroux and Peter McLaren, "Teacher Education and the Politics of Engagement," *Harvard Educational Review* (August 1986). p. 235.

14. Cited in Giroux, H. A., and Peter McLaren, "Teacher Education."

15. Giroux and McLaren, "Teacher Education."

16. Donald, *Language, Literacy and Schooling*.

17. J. Cummings, "Functional Language Proficiency in Context," in *Significant Instructional Features in Bilingual Education*, ed. W. Tikunoff (San Francisco, Calif.: Far West Laboratory, 1984).

18. Roger Fowler et al., *Language and Control* (London: Routledge & Kegan Paul, 1979), p. 192.

19. Greg Myers, "Reality, Concensus, and Reform in the Rhetoric of Composition Teaching," *College English* 48, no. 2 (February 1986).

20. Kozol, p. 4.

21. J. Anthony Lukas, *Common Ground* (New York: Alfred A. Knopf, 1985), p. 282.

22. Ibid., p. 138.

23. Walmsley, "Purpose and Content," p. 84.

24. Giroux, *Theory and Resistance*. p. 226.

25. Ibid. p. 226.

26. Walmsley, "Purpose and Content," p. 84.

Bibliography

Bakhtin, M. *The Dialogic Imagination: Four Essays*, as quoted in Harold Rosen, "The Importance of Story," *Language Arts* 63 (1986): 234.

Bennett, W. *New York Times*, September 26 and 27, 1985.

Bourdieu, P., and J. C. Passeron, *Reproduction in Education, Society, and Culture*. Beverly Hills, Calif.: Sage, 1977.

Caetano, J. *Boletim da Sociedade de Geografia*. 3rd series. Lisbon, n.d.

Cummings, J. "Functional Language Proficiency in Context: Classroom Participation as an Interactive Process." In *Significant Instructional Features in Bilingual Education: Proceedings of Symposium at NABE 1983*, edited by W. Tikunoff. San Francisco, Calif.: Far West Laboratory, 1984.

Donald, J. *Language, Literacy and Schooling*. London: Open University Press, in press.

Fowler, Roger et al. *Language and Control*. London: Routledge & Kegan Paul, 1979.

Freire, P. *Pedagogy in Process*. New York: Seabury Press, 1978.

Giroux, H. A. *Theory and Resistance: A Pedagogy for the Opposition*. South Hadley, Mass.: J. F. Bergin Publishers, 1983.

Giroux, H. A., and Peter McLaren. "Teacher Education and the Politics of Engagement: The Case for Democratic Schooling." *Harvard Educational Review*, (August 1986).

Kenneth, J. "The Sociology of Pierre Bourdieu." *Educational Review* 25 (1973).

Lukas, J. Anthony. *Common Ground*. New York: Alfred A. Knopf, 1985.

Myers, Greg. "Reality, Concensus, and Reform in the Rhetoric of Composition Teaching." *College English* 48, no. 2 (February 1986).

Rosenblatt, L. "The Enriching Values of Reading." In *Reading in an Age of Mass Communication*, edited by William S. Gray. New York: Appleton-Century Crofts, 1949.

UNESCO. *An Asian Model of Educational Development: Perspectives for 1965-1980*. Paris: UNESCO, 1966.

Walmsley, S. "On the Purpose and Content of Secondary Reading Programs: Educational Ideological Perspectives." *Curriculum Inquiry* 11 (1981).

Index